Hacking Gender and Technology in Journalism

Hacking Gender and Technology in Journalism addresses the question of whether journalism's new digital spaces suffer from the same gendered structures as traditional media organisations, or whether they go beyond such bias.

This book offers insights into the challenges that women journalists face in relation to technological innovation, as well as the potential for developing strategies for empowerment that it offers. More specifically, there is a focus on the gendering of digital skills, the construction of gender in new digital spheres of journalism, and how these changes can lead to the disruption of gender inequalities in journalism.

This book will be of interest to scholars in multimedia journalism, media ethics, and gender studies.

Sara De Vuyst is a postdoctoral researcher at the Department of Communication Studies at Ghent University. Her research interests are feminist media studies and, more specifically, gender issues and technological innovation journalism. She has a passion for feminism and a strong interest in digital storytelling, data journalism, and innovative journalistic formats. De Vuyst is vice-chair of the ECREA Gender and Communication section and part of a network of research on gendered online harassment.

Disruptions: Studies in Digital Journalism

Series editor: Bob Franklin

Disruptions refers to the radical changes provoked by the affordances of digital technologies that occur at a pace and on a scale that disrupts settled understandings and traditional ways of creating value, interacting and communicating both socially and professionally. The consequences for digital journalism involve far reaching changes to business models, professional practices, roles, ethics, products and even challenges to the accepted definitions and understandings of journalism. For Digital Journalism Studies, the field of academic inquiry which explores and examines digital journalism, disruption results in paradigmatic and tectonic shifts in scholarly concerns. It prompts reconsideration of research methods, theoretical analyses and responses (oppositional and consensual) to such changes, which have been described as being akin to 'a moment of mind-blowing uncertainty'.

Routledge's new book series, ***Disruptions: Studies in Digital Journalism***, seeks to capture, examine and analyse these moments of exciting and explosive professional and scholarly innovation which characterize developments in the day-to-day practice of journalism in an age of digital media, and which are articulated in the newly emerging academic discipline of Digital Journalism Studies.

Making NonProfit News
Market Models, Influence and Journalistic Practice
Patrick Ferrucci

Conceptualizing Immersive Journalism
Ana Luisa Sánchez Laws

Hacking Gender and Technology in Journalism
Sara De Vuyst

For more information, please visit: www.routledge.com/Disruptions/book-series/DISRUPTDIGJOUR

Hacking Gender and Technology in Journalism

Sara De Vuyst

Routledge
Taylor & Francis Group
LONDON AND NEW YORK

First published 2020
by Routledge
4 Park Square, Milton Park, Abingdon, Oxon OX14 4RN

and by Routledge
605 Third Avenue, New York, NY 10017

First issued in paperback 2022

Routledge is an imprint of the Taylor & Francis Group, an informa business

Publisher's Note
The publisher has gone to great lengths to ensure the quality of this reprint but points out that some imperfections in the original copies may be apparent.

British Library Cataloguing-in-Publication Data
A catalogue record for this book is available from the British Library

Library of Congress Cataloging-in-Publication Data
A catalog record for this book has been requested

ISBN 13: 978-1-03-247482-3 (pbk)
ISBN 13: 978-0-367-20528-7 (hbk)
ISBN 13: 978-0-429-26202-9 (ebk)

DOI: 10.4324/9780429262029

Typeset in Times New Roman
by Apex CoVantage, LLC

Contents

Acknowledgements

I would like to thank all journalists and technologists who have participated in my interviews for taking the time to talk to me and sharing their experiences.

A special thanks goes to Mariana Santos for inviting me to Stanford University and introducing me to Chicas Poderosas. Your enthusiasm about the empowerment of women and the energy of Chicas Poderosas is truly inspiring. Thank you, Luisa Ortiz Pérez, for your advice on self-care and feminist strategies for researching online gender-based violence.

It was always a pleasure to participate in the Dataharvest conference and learn about new trends, tools and topics in data journalism. Thank you, Brigitte Alfter and Ides Debruyne, for organising and welcoming me at the event, sharing your knowledge on data journalism and introducing me to your colleagues.

I would like to express my thanks to Maria Edström and Monika Djerf-Pierre for the valuable feedback during my visit to Gothenburg University. I appreciate all the tips and connections that you shared with me. I came back from the research stay with many new ideas to start working on my book.

Thank you, Marie Germis and Julie Persyn, for your help with conducting interviews for the research on online harassment in journalism.

This book would not have been possible without the Routledge team. Thank you, Jennifer Vennall and Margaret Farrelly, for being there for me in every step of the process. Special thanks to the editor of the series, Bob Franklin, for the opportunity to work on this project and for the feedback throughout the writing of the book.

Introduction

Hacking Gender and Technology in Journalism explores the gender dimensions of technological innovations in journalism. The word 'hacking' in the title serves as a guideline throughout the book. Its multiple layers of meaning will be addressed in the different chapters. Even though hacking is often associated with computers and cyber criminality, it also refers to detecting lacks in a system and finding new, unforeseen ways to deal with them.

Feminism provides a lens that illustrates how gender inequality is actually a bug in the system of journalism. In news production, there are significant gender gaps in pay, recruitment, allocation of work and promotion that cannot be justified by differences in skill or quality of work. Even though the number of female journalists has drawn closer to the number of male journalists, they do not have equal opportunities to participate in decision-making and contribute to news content. Moreover, the claim that news media provide accurate, fair and balanced reporting that includes a diversity of voices is not met, since women are significantly underrepresented and portrayed stereotypically in the news. Gender bias, both in news content and production, prevents journalism from serving its audiences and fulfilling its core tasks of informing citizens and representing diverse opinions. It is a deficiency in how journalism operates and a loss to society and democracy because it diminishes the quality and representativeness of news (Adams, 2018; Edström, 2014; Tuchman, 1978).

In the last few decades, an increase in female journalists has run in parallel with technological transitions in the media industry. Digitalisation has not only played a role in changes in media structures and working conditions in journalism, but also altered the news-gathering and production process. On the one hand, it has introduced a wide range of digital tools and platforms for gathering and disseminating news. On the other hand, in an increasingly digitalised context, new technologically-driven forms of journalism have emerged. It is interesting to observe that trends in gender and technology are commonly studied separately. Feminist media scholars have widely documented obstacles that limit the opportunities of women in traditional media organisations, but studies rarely take into account technological changes. In journalism studies, digitalisation is often cited as one of the most significant trends in the media industry but mostly approached through a gender-neutral lens. Although the literature on the adoption of technology and the increased interaction between journalism and technology is growing rapidly, gender issues are usually not part of the discussion.

These are, without a doubt, fascinating developments for researchers, students and practitioners of journalism. Regarding gender, however, the key question remains: are these new digital spaces of journalism still characterised by gendered and patriarchal structures as their predecessor and traditional media organisations or do they go beyond gender, create opportunities for women and provide areas where journalists can navigate free from gender and other biases? The answer to this question, as we will see in the next chapters, lies somewhere in the middle of such binary propositions.

Gender and technology

In discussions of both technology and gender, progress is frequently presented as unavoidable and continuous. Moreover, even though technological innovation has played a significant role in shaping the global media industry, its transformative capacity tends to be exaggerated for ideological purposes. A strong focus on technology creates a sense of inevitability or determinism around changes that are taking place in journalistic labour, while corporate interests – which are the real drivers of work intensification, precarious working conditions and flexible employment contracts – remain out of the picture (Compton, 2009). In a similar way, gender advancement is generally described as a consecutive process, mostly based on beliefs that an increase of women in newsrooms will automatically result in less gender bias in the work environment and news output or that the endpoint is reached and the glass ceiling is broken when a few women make it to decision-making positions (Eisenstein, 1981; Gallagher, 1995; Mills, 1997). Both views take societal structures for granted and result in the assumption that improvement will be achieved without dealing with underlying reasons for inequality (Adam, 2005).

Previous research, however, has shown that the progress of women in journalism is far from linear and profoundly sensitive to structural transitions in media industries. In many countries, the increase of female journalists occurred simultaneously with a trend toward the commercialisation of news. This concurrence is typically (but falsely) interpreted as causality in which the recruitment of women is seen as the reason for changes in news content (Harp, 2008). The shift to more human interest, infotainment and personification is sometimes even labelled as the feminisation of news, which gives the increasing numbers of women in the profession a negative connotation because of an implicit association with a decrease in the standards and credibility of journalism. This analysis is blind to the growing concentration and conglomeration of media companies and the strategies for maximising profit and advertising revenues that are in fact changing the news and threatening the quality and plurality of journalism (McChesney, 2004).

Media consolidation also has a negative impact on women's opportunities and media ownership since it tends to centralise the power in the hands of an even smaller, privileged male elite (Byerly, 2014). Moreover changes in the news industry are experienced differently by journalists based on gender, with intensified work regimes and neoliberal practices disproportionally affecting female journalists and possibly reversing efforts to create more inclusive newsrooms (North, 2009). These are likely reasons why the percentage of female journalists that increased considerably in the final decades of the twentieth century and the beginning of the twenty-first century is now showing signs of stagnation (Weaver & Wu, 1998; Weaver & Wilnat, 2012; GMMP, 2015). Keeping in mind the precariousness and instability of the advancement to gender equality and the close connection with structural transitions in the profession, it essential to monitor how recent digital shifts in the news industry relate to gender developments.

From digital disruption to gender disruption

Innovation is typically associated with some kind of change, transformation, alteration, revolution or disruption. This means that new spaces in journalism are not innovative if they reproduce the same unequal structures as previous ones. Moreover, the full capacity of technology is not used if it is only embraced by a privileged group of journalists. Gender and other forms of diversity are essential drivers of innovation because they encourage the inclusion of different perspectives and experiences (European Commission, 2018; Hewlett, Marshall, & Sherbin, 2013). That is why digital disruption has to be accompanied by a feminist rethinking of journalism to eliminate power structures and remove barriers that are limiting journalists from reaching their full potential and creativity.

Feminism offers insights into how forms of bias are legitimised and the gender status quo is maintained in journalism. Just like the transformative power of technology is exaggerated for ideological purposes, differences between male and female journalists are often magnified and portrayed as natural in a way that presents inequality as inevitable. My position in this book is aimed at going beyond determinism in terms of gender, technology and the relationship between the two. This means that gender is not seen as a fixed attribute, but rather as constructed through social practices and interaction, while technological innovation is considered not only a matter of organisational factors, but also of the individual agency and decisions of journalists.

Regarding the relationship between the two, I will focus on how gender and technology are mutually shaped and on how people working in journalism and technology give meaning to gender and the impact of technological innovation in their lives, construct their attitudes and perceptions toward gender and technology and experience structures that limit their opportunities. However, in the same way that technology cannot be considered the sole driver of change in journalism, gender does not relate and unravel the entire story of inequality. Experiences and subject positions are not only shaped by gender but also by interactions with other social identities such as sexuality, age or ethnicity. Although my analysis will mainly focus on gender inequality, it also tries to take into account these other possible intersections to provide a deeper understanding of inequalities in journalism.

A framework for hacking

My framework for hacking gender in journalism will have a theoretical and empirical component. Chapter 1 addresses the gender–technology question in journalism by bringing together insights from three fields of inquiry. From feminist media studies, I draw on research that exposes gendered obstacles such as the glass ceiling, the old boys' network, sexism and sexual harassment that contribute to the underrepresentation of women in decision-making positions, higher age groups, and prestigious hard news beats and media sectors. This is combined with insights from journalism studies concerning structural transitions in the media industry, changing working conditions in journalism, the adoption of technology in the newsroom, and new forms of data-driven and computational journalism. Even though research on gender and digitalisation in journalism is still being established, in feminist technology studies, the relationship between technology and gender has long been debated and conceptualised. There is a rich body of literature on the underrepresentation of women in information and communication technology (ICT) industries and education, gender differences in the adoption and consumption of digital technologies, and gendered identities in cyberspace. Considering the increased importance of ICT in journalism, I found these insights valuable to apply to my research on gender and technology in journalism.

In line with the feminist aim and ambition, the book will provide conceptual building blocks but also create a basis or foundation for change. Feminist theory not only offers the tools to illustrate why patriarchy and other forms of dominance are a problem for journalism but also how gender discrimination is sustained, as well as the ways in which structures of oppression can be challenged and transformed. The subsequent four chapters draw on qualitative interview research to explore different aspects of the relationship between gender and technology. Between February 2015 and May 2019, 60 interviews were conducted with journalism professionals from different countries and regions including Europe (42), the United States (10), Latin America (6) and Africa (2). The selection criteria were distinctive reflecting the particular topic of study and will be explained as the various chapters unravel.

The first step toward hacking the gender gap is to expose the subtle and invisible ways in which technological innovation in journalism creates gendered challenges. For this reason, Chapter 2 focuses on how digital skills are gendered in journalism. Several gendered obstacles related to technology such as the 'geek' stereotype, the coding ceiling, and an intensification of work-family conflicts are discussed, drawing on interviews with journalists with varying levels of digital expertise. In Chapter 3, I examine gender and the development of new digital spaces for journalism. More specifically, there is a focus on data journalism. Data journalism is exemplary of increased interaction between journalism and the technology field, which makes it a compelling case to look at from a gender perspective. I talked to journalists and technologists who are involved in data journalism about their motivations for entering the field, career trajectories, work practices and issues related to gender and diversity.

Chapter 4 addresses the ways in which female journalists are actively challenging the obstacles that were described in previous chapters and provides examples of empowerment through technology. Several initiatives and good practices aimed at closing the gender gap in journalism and technology are explored. These are combined with insights from interviews with journalism professionals who are involved in these initiatives as well as colleagues who are not familiar yet with them. Chapter 5 builds on these ideas to examine possible forms of resistance and backlash to strategies for empowerment. It focuses on how traditional forms of gender bias appear in modified ways in digital spaces, and more specifically, on online harassment of journalists. Interviews with journalists and columnists who have been confronted with online abuse offer insights into consequences, coping strategies and parallels with offline forms of sexual harassment.

The concluding chapter integrates the experiences of interviewees into a structural framework for change. It offers an analysis of the future of gender in journalism and formulates recommendations for combatting sexism and bias in the media industry. The focus is on how to create a climate in journalism that can lead to disruption of gender inequality as well as forms of backlash that are emerging in digital spaces and can cause setbacks. This final chapter also offers certain reservations and caveats concerning the general conclusions and limitations of the research and provides suggestions for further study.

Conceptual building blocks

Bourdieu's field theory, and in particular, appropriations by feminist researchers, are used as conceptual building blocks in this book. The concepts of capital, habitus and doxa have proved fruitful in gaining insights into gender relations in journalism (Djerf-Pierre, 2005, 2007; Melin, 2008; Tsui & Lee, 2012; Zuiderveld, 2011). I also found them useful in gaining understandings of the value of digital skills, the development of new spaces or subfields and strategies for challenging and reproducing gender inequality in journalism. Bourdieu's approach to gender as a social construction and a system of power fits well with my aim to go beyond gender essentialism and biological determinism (Bourdieu, 2001). Moreover, his concepts support an analysis that takes into account the ways in which different social categories can amplify or weaken each other in the social world, which is in line with the goal to look beyond gender as a single category of privilege or disadvantage.

Bourdieu's field theory allows us to understand journalism as a (semi-) autonomous social field in social space with its own culture and logic (Benson, 1999; Bourdieu & Wacquant, 1996). Those rules of the field called doxa consist of implicit schemes based on couples of opposition (Dick, 2008). Values and processes are considered doxic when they are perceived as natural and legitimate. In journalism, doxa refers to the taken-for-granted assumptions about journalistic practices, values, and qualities. Authors have noted that the doxa of journalism is based on a gendered logic, which is based on a belief system that associates femininity with low status and masculinity with high status. This becomes evident, for example, in the division of news beats into male-dominated prestigious hard news topics and female-dominated as less prestigious soft news topics (Melin, 2008).

An important dynamic in a field is the distribution of different kinds of resources or capital (Thompson, 2008). Bourdieu (1986) refers to economic, cultural and social capital. Economic capital encompasses money and property rights. Social capital includes family relationships and support from formal and informal networks. Cultural capital refers to taste patterns, knowledge, and skills. All of these forms of capital can be transformed into symbolic capital if they are perceived and recognised as legitimate in a specific field. Thus, symbolic capital refers to status, authority and prestige (Webb, Shirato, & Danaher, 2002). Although Bourdieu initially only distinguishes these four types, he encourages the addition of new forms of capital. Digital capital and gender capital, which were added more recently by other scholars, will be central in this book and will be discussed more in detail in the next paragraph.

All together, the forms of capital produce the habitus which has both a structured and a structuring component (Bourdieu, 1990). The 'structured' part of habitus refers to a system of social dispositions that is formed through processes of socialisation during which external, social structures are internalised (Schwartz, 1997). The 'structuring' part refers to the idea that the habitus tends to structure actions or practices. In *Masculine Domination*, Bourdieu (2001) describes the habitus as gendered, with each gender occupying a distinct "sexually characterised habitus" (p. 3). What this means is that men and women are socialised differently in line with socially and culturally appropriate gender behaviours and norms (McCall, 1992). For Bourdieu (2001), habitus is key to understanding why women, who form a subordinated group and are disadvantaged in this system, accept the male-dominated order. Through habitus, their perceptions and thoughts are structured in a way that corresponds with the prevailing gender order, and their aspirations and actions will mainly confirm their subordinate position. By presenting social gender divisions as doxic, Bourdieu (2001) leaves little room for changes.

Gender and digital capital

Feminist researchers have extensively reworked the concepts of Bourdieu to create more room for resistance. While Bourdieu used the idea of capital primarily to examine class advantage, it also proved to be useful for investigating gender advantage (Huppatz, 2012; Lovell, 2000; Ross-Smith & Huppatz, 2010; Skeggs, 2004). McCall (1992), for example, understands gender as a form of capital based on Bourdieu's statement that cultural capital refers to embodied dispositions. Moi (1991), however, does not consider gender as a pure form of capital on its own because it does not have its own field. According to her, gender is connected to symbolic capital because it is dependent on perceptions and evaluations, which are patterned by cultural beliefs about gender. Moi (1991) assumes that in most contexts, maleness functions as positive and femaleness functions as negative symbolic capital. This is in line with Bourdieu's statement (2001) that "women are separated from men by a negative symbolic coefficient which . . . negatively affects everything that they are and do" (p. 93). Furthermore, Moi (1999) notes that women can compensate for their negative symbolic gender capital by gaining other forms of capital, which creates more agency and possibilities for changing positions.

In addition to the adjustments to Bourdieu's concept of capital made by feminist researchers, other authors have updated Bourdieu's original formulation based on the changes in ICT by introducing the idea of digital capital. Paino and Renzulli (2012), for example, have expanded Bourdieu's (1986) traditional conceptualisation of cultural capital because they believe that computer competence and knowledge are essential in today's information society. Similarly, Tondeur, Sinnaeve, van Houtte and van Braak (2010) added that the attitudes, use and competence regarding ICT should also be seen as indicators of cultural capital. The interaction between gender and digital capital will be a common thread in this book. Every empirical chapter will highlight a different aspect of the relationship between these types of capital.

References

Adam, A. (2005). *Gender, ethics, and information technology*. Hampshire, UK: Palgrave Macmillan.

Adams, C. (2018). They go for gender first: The nature and effect of sexist abuse of female technology journalists. *Journalism Practice*, *12*(7), 850–869.

Benson, R. (1999). Field theory in comparative context: A new paradigm for media studies. *Theory and Society*, *28*(3), 463–498.

Bourdieu, P. (1986). The forms of capital. In R. Richardson (Ed.), *Handbook of theory and research for sociology of education* (pp. 241–258). New York, NY: Greenwood.

Bourdieu, P. (1990). *The logic of practice*. Cambridge and Oxford, UK: Polity Press.

Bourdieu, P. (2001). *Masculine domination*. Cambridge, UK: Polity Press.

Bourdieu, P., & Wacquant, L. J. (1996). *An invitation to reflexive sociology*. Cambridge, UK: Polity Press.

Byerly, C. M. (2014). Media conglomeration and women's interests: A global concern. *Feminist Media Studies*, *14*(2), 322–326.

Compton, J. R. (2009). Newspapers, labor and the flux of economic uncertainty. In S. Allan (Ed.), *The Routledge companion to news and journalism studies* (pp. 591–601). New York, NY: Routledge.

Dick, P. (2008). Resistance, gender, and Bourdieu's notion of the field. *Management Communication Quarterly*, *21*(3), 327–343.

Djerf-Pierre, M. (2005). Lonely at the top: Gendered media elites in Sweden. *Journalism*, *6*(3), 265–290.

Djerf-Pierre, M. (2007). The gender of journalism: The structure and logic of the field in the twentieth century. *Nordicom Review*, *28*(jubilee issue), 81–104.

Edström, M. (2014). Nordic journalism with gender parity and problems. In M. Edström & R. Molster (Eds.), *Making change: Nordic examples of working towards gender inequality in the media* (pp. 47–52). Göteborg, Sweden: Nordicom.

Eisenstein, Z. (1981). *The radical future of liberal feminism*. New York, NY: Longman.

European Commission (2018). *Women in the digital age*. Retrieved from http://ec.europa.eu/newsroom/dae/document.cfm?doc_id=50224

Gallagher, M. (1995). *An unfinished story: Gender patterns in media employment*. Paris, France: UNESCO.

GMMP (2015). *Who makes the news? Global Media Monitoring Project*. London, UK: World Association for Christian Communication.

Harp, D. (2008). News, feminist theories, and the gender divide. In P. Pointdexter, S. Meraz, & A. Schmitz Weiss (Eds.), *Women, men, and news: Divided and disconnected in the news media landscape* (pp. 265–279). Oxon, UK and New York, NY: Routledge.

Hewlett, S. A., Marshall, M. M., & Sherbin, S. (2013, December). *How diversity can drive innovation*. Retrieved from https://hbr.org/2013/12/how-diversity-can-drive-innovation#

Huppatz, K. (2012). *Gender capital at work: Intersections of femininity, masculinity, class and occupation*. London, UK: Palgrave Macmillan.

Lovell, T. (2000). Thinking feminism with and against Bourdieu. *Feminist Theory*, *1*(1), 11–32.

McCall, L. (1992). Does gender fit? Bourdieu, feminism, and conceptions of social order. *Theory and Society*, *21*(6), 837–867.

McChesney, R. W. (2004). *The problem of the media*. New York, NY: Monthly Review Books.

Melin, M. (2008). *Gendered journalism cultures: Strategies and tactics in the field of journalism in Britain and Sweden* (Unpublished doctoral dissertation), University of Göteborg, Göteborg, Sweden.

Mills, K. (1997). What difference do women journalists make? In P. Norris (Ed.), *Women, media, and politics* (pp. 41–50). Oxford, UK and New York, NY: Oxford University Press.

Moi, T. (1991). Appropriating Bourdieu: Feminist theory and Pierre Bourdieu's sociology of culture. *New Literary History*, *22*(4), 1017–1049.

Moi, T. (1999). *What is a woman?* Oxford, UK: Oxford University Press.

North, L. (2009). *The gendered newsroom: How journalists experience the changing world of media*. Cresskill, NJ: Hampton Press.

Paino, M., & Renzulli, L. A. (2012). Digital dimension of cultural capital: The (in)visible advantages for students who exhibit computer skills. *Sociology of Education*, *86*(2), 124–138.

Ross-Smith, A., & Huppatz, K. (2010). Management, women and gender capital. *Gender, Work & Organization*, *17*(5), 547–567.

Schwartz, D. (1997). *Culture and power: The sociology of Pierre Bourdieu*. Chicago, IL: University of Chicago Press.

Skeggs, B. (2004). Introducing Pierre Bourdieu's analysis of class, gender and sexuality. In L. Adkins & B. Skeggs (Eds.), *Feminism after Bourdieu* (pp. 19–33). Oxford, UK: Blackwell.

Thompson, P. (2008). Field. In M. Grenfell (Ed.), *Pierre Bourdieu: Key concepts* (pp. 67–81). Durham, UK: Acumen Publishing Limited.

Tondeur, J., Sinnaeve, I., van Houtte, M., & van Braak, J. (2010). ICT as cultural capital: The relationship between socioeconomic status and the computer-use of young people. *New Media & Society*, *13*(1), 151–168.

Tsui, C. Y. S., & Lee, F. L. F. (2012). Trajectories of women journalists' career in Hong Kong. *Journalism Studies*, *13*(3), 370–385.

Tuchman, G. (1978). *Making news: A study in the construction of reality*. New York, NY: Free Press.

Weaver, D. H., & Wilnat, L. (2012). *The global journalist in the 21st century*. New York, NY: Routledge.

Weaver, D. H., & Wu, W. (1998). *The global journalist: News people around the world*. Cresskill, NJ: Hampton Press.

Webb, J., Schirato, T., & Danaher, G. (2002). *Understanding Bourdieu*. London, UK: Sage.

Zuiderveld, M. (2011). Hitting the glass ceiling – Gender and media management in Sub-Saharan Africa. *Journal of African Media Studies*, *3*(3), 401–415.

1 Tackling the gender–technology relationship in journalism

This chapter offers a state-of-the-art of research on gender, journalism and technology. The aim is to hack an important gap in the literature, being the lack of explorations of the gender dimensions of technological innovation in journalism. In doing so, it connects the dots between feminist media studies, journalism studies and feminist technology studies. It is important to note that hacking in this context does not imply discarding previous scholarly work and starting from a completely blank slate, but rather, it stands for illustrating how the insights of these three fields of inquiry can complement each other to tackle the gender–technology question in journalism.

Hacking feminist media studies

When conducting research aimed at disrupting gender inequalities in journalism, it is essential to begin from an awareness of previous questions, methodologies and knowledge raised by feminist academics, activists and journalists. This is not only because to overlook their accomplishments would contribute to the exclusion of women's voices and perspectives from the public and academic debate but also because gender barriers that appear to be novel often turn out to be a modification of previously documented limitations. Struggles experienced in feminist activism have a tendency of repeating themselves over time.

Consider #MeToo, a hashtag that was used by numerous women, also in media professions, to share experiences of sexual harassment which sparked a debate that shook the industry to its core. This movement has many parallels with the work of second-wave feminists in the 1960s and 1970s aimed at putting women's individual experiences of sexual harassment on the public agenda. #MeToo turned the personal into the political in a few clicks and created alternative spaces to tell stories that are usually untold in the mainstream media. However, just like in the 1960s and 1970s, several dynamics were set in motion to break the momentum of the movement. Women who shared their experiences were discredited in some cases and the legitimation of allegations was questioned, which can prevent people from speaking up on future occasions. Knowledge of the history of feminist movements increases awareness of the possibility of backlash in the struggle for empowerment.

This book can draw on a rich tradition of feminist media studies in which different aspects of the relationship between gender and media are critically explored (Bachmann, Harp, & Loke, 2018). Questions of gender and media representation, production and reception were put on the scholarly and political agenda by feminist academics and activists starting in the 1970s (Byerly, 2018). The link between feminist theory, research and activism has been a common thread since the early days of this field (Gallagher, 2001). Interests met in the desire to go further than constructing new knowledge, produce social change and disrupt the gender status quo. Views, however, differed on what disruption should look like and how it should be achieved. This is explored further in Chapter 4, where I critically reflect on perspectives on gendered changes in journalism and position the results of my research on gender and technology within these debates.

From on the screen to behind the scenes

The representation of women and men in news media was a focal point of the newly formed coalitions between feminist activists and academics. Quantitative media monitoring was used to criticise media companies for not including women in the news and exposed the magnitude of this problem (Gallagher, 2001). The Global Media Monitoring Project (1995), which analysed the presence and portrayal of women and men by news outlets in 71 countries, is exemplary of this type of research. This study demonstrated two global patterns in news content: women were strongly under-represented, and, when they made the news, they were mostly portrayed in a stereotypical manner. Since 1995, the project has been repeated every five years in a growing number of countries (GMMP, 2000, 2005, 2010, 2015).

To the present, the lion's share of feminist media scholarship centres on media content, but beginning in the 1980s, attention shifted toward what happens behind the scenes in news production where decisions about content are made (Byerly, 2013; North, 2009). Parallel to initial research on representation, early studies on production used quantitative methods to gather statistics on the employment of women and men in different media genres and countries (Burks & Stone, 1993; Demoor, Saeys, De Bleeckere, Reymenants, & De Clercq, 2000; Diekerhof, Acker, Elias, & Sax, 1986; Lünenborg, 1997). A large number of these studies focused specifically on the news media and were supported by international bodies such as the

European Commission, UNESCO and the United Nations (European Commission, 1991, 1999; Gallagher, 1981, 1982, 1984, 1987, 1995a, 1995b; Holman, 1992; Holman & Ortiz, 1992). The results, however, were often not comparable because of a lack of consistency in the definition of journalists and in the variables which were measured. Gallagher's study (1995a), *An Unfinished Story: Gender Patterns in Media Employment,* offered the first comparative overview of women's employment in media industries in 41 countries and 239 organisations. Several other international surveys provided an updated account of this landmark study (Byerly, 2011; EIGE, 2013; Fröhlich & Lafky, 2008). The numbers gathered in these surveys show that the structure of journalism employment is marked by three gendered patterns.

Three main gender divides

The first divide runs through the participation of women and men in the journalistic workforce. An abundant amount of research indicates that women are underrepresented in journalism. Gallagher's study in 1995 revealed that women's engagement in media employment constituted on average less than one third (32%). More than a decade later, a study of the International Women's Media Foundation (IWMF) in nearly 60 countries found an almost identical percentage of women in the full-time journalism workforce (33%) (Byerly, 2011). These averages do not say anything about outliers and countries that are performing significantly better or worse regarding women's access to the journalistic workforce, but they do offer insight into a generally gendered pattern and evolving trends across time. Moreover, the gender divide in the participation in journalism employment intersects with age. The male to female ratio tends to be more balanced in younger age groups, but the percentage of women steadily declines as age increases (Delano, 2003; Franks, 2013; Hollings, Lealand, Samson, & Tilley, 2007).

Second, the engagement of women reflects the type of professional position and the power associated with it. Women are commonly underrepresented in decision-making positions and technical positions (Bulkeley, 2004; Hemlinger, 2001; Ross & Carter, 2011; WMC, 2019). This gendered pattern is referred to as vertical gender segregation. A study of the European Institute for Gender Equality (EIGE) (2013) in the European Union member states showed that women represent only one third (30%) at all levels of leadership in media organisations. When looking in more detail at the type of positions, women make up 16% of the CEOs, 21% of Chief Operating Officer positions and 25% of board members. In the IWMF's study, the global percentage of women in senior management positions was slightly higher than one third (39%). Vertical segregation also occurs in countries with gender parity in journalistic ranks, such as Sweden and Finland (Byerly, 2013). The absence at the macro-level of media ownership implies that women are not present in positions where they can make a difference to decision-making (Nicholson, 2007; Ross, 2014). Financial resources and the power to define hiring procedures and policies remain the privilege of a male elite (Byerly, 2004). Because women are clustered in lower positions with limited chances for advancement, their career progress is much slower when compared to male journalists (Hemlinger, Linton, & Smith, 2002).

The underrepresentation of women in decision-making positions is closely related to the gendered division of tasks, also referred to as horizontal segregation (Pointdexter & Harp, 2008; van Zoonen, 1994). Status is an important explanatory factor for the segregation of news beats and media sectors along gender lines. Scholars have shed light on the gendered nature of the soft news – hard news binary. As early as 1973, Tuchman's ethnographic work indicated how news is classified based on a dichotomy in which hard news has a higher level of newsworthiness and publishing priority than soft news. In her later work, she draws attention to a gendered layer in this distinction by connecting the difference to stereotypical assumptions about men and women (Tuchman, 1978). Women work more in soft news beats that are typically associated with lower status such as human interest stories, health, fashion and education, whereas men work more in hard news beats such as political news, business news and investigative journalism that are associated with high status (Chambers & Steiner, 2010; Franks, 2013; GMMP, 2015; North, 2016b; WMC, 2019). Men are also dominant in sports journalism. A second axis of horizontal segregation refers to gender differences in employment in media sectors. Women are underrepresented in media sectors associated with high status such as the newspapers and press agencies but have made more progress in the audio-visual and magazine sector that are typically associated with lower status (Christmas, 2008; Delano, 2003).

Beyond the body count

Although quantification is valuable to expose the gender division of journalistic labour, there is a growing awareness that counting women and men is little more than "scratching the surface of the realities of media" (de Bruin, 2000, p. 225). To gain a comprehensive picture of gender inequalities in journalism, scholarship has to go beyond the body count and focus on "specific social practices, embodied in conventions and rules, formally and informally, based on history and tradition" (de Bruin, 2000, p. 225). This shift offers a deeper understanding of the gendered nature of newsrooms and allows us to explain where and how gender is meaningful.

Qualitative research methods such as in-depth interviews and ethnography are increasingly used to uncover obstacles that sustain gender patterns. This shift in research design went hand-in-hand with a change in the focus on 'women' as a central research category to the notion of 'gender'. Counting merely offers a snapshot that puts men and women into two static, homogenous groups based on manifest characteristics and biological differences. Although these studies cannot grasp the complexity of gender in journalism, there is considerable merit in the ability to track trends through time, make comparisons between countries and spark public debates on gender inequality in the media.

Going beyond the body count means leaving behind thinking in terms of binaries. This shift is inspired by the concept of 'doing gender' introduced by West and Zimmerman (1987) that positions gender as continually produced and reproduced in social activities and practices rather than a fixed and natural attribute. Gender is approached as a social process through which social and latent cultural meanings are attributed to biological differences between men and women. In organisational sociology, this way of thinking is applied to how gender operates in work organisations. Gender is not only considered a variable imported from outside the organisation anymore but also something that is actively constructed in organisational processes.

The flexible and dynamic character of gender is the guiding principle of Joan Acker's (1992) theory of gendered organisations. She was one of the first scholars who theorised organisations as gendered and explains that this means that "advantage and disadvantage, exploitation and control, action and emotion, meaning and identity, are patterned through and in terms of a distinction between male and female, masculine and feminine" (Acker, 1990, p. 85). Her theory identifies several interacting processes through which gendering happens in work contexts. These ideas were applied to journalism to study how gender is "done" in news organisations. Acker's theory provides a useful analytical tool to examine gendered substructures in newsrooms in the next sections.

Gendered newsrooms

Through interaction between processes of structure, culture, interaction and identity, gender is embedded in news organisations and becomes part of the social fabric (de Bruin, 1999). As described in the previous section, the structure of news organisations is characterised by a gendered division of labour. Jobs and tasks in journalism are gender typed or permeated by assumptions about gender and associated with masculinity or femininity (Löfgren-Nilsson, 2010). This gendered structure is both translated into and sustained by the organisational culture of newsrooms. These are values, assumptions, understandings, symbols and norms that are shared by journalists and consciously or unconsciously influence their behaviour.

Feminist scholars highlight the importance of looking from a gender perspective when they describe newsroom culture as 'blokey' and ego-driven (North, 2012), exclusionary (Elmore, 2007), macho (Ross & Carter, 2011), masculine (Kim, 2006), patriarchal (Robinson, 2005) or "organized around a man-as-norm and woman-as-interloper structure" (Ross, 2001, p. 533). These researchers also note that assumptions about gender are so deeply embedded that journalists are not conscious of the influence on their behaviour, language, and patterns of social interaction. Newsroom culture is rarely questioned because it "masquerades as a neutral 'professional ethos'" (Ross, 2001, p. 533).

Feminist research is aimed at making the invisible visible and revealing how values, beliefs and journalistic routines that seem gender-neutral are disproportionally disadvantageous for female journalists. An example of this is work expectations that are based on the assumption that news never stops, which results in the idea that journalists have to be available 24/7 (de Bruin, 1999). This requirement of around-the-clock availability translates into irregular and long work hours (Aldridge, 2001). Van Zoonen (1994) questions whether this demand, which journalists consider as an inevitable part of the job, is an absolute organisational necessity when she points out that this is "a product of professional mythology" (p. 53).

Considering that household and care tasks are still divided based on traditional gender patterns, this demand is typically more accessible for male journalists who can count on the support of a female partner than for female journalists who carry a disproportionate share of the household and care labour (Franks, 2013). This combination creates a double burden or a second shift for women (Hochschild, 1997). The incompatibility of journalism with motherhood is a frequently cited reason explaining why women leave the profession or intend to do so early in their career (Everbach & Flournoy, 2007; Hardin, Shain, & Poniatowski, 2008; Reinardy, 2009; Stone, 2000). It can partly explain why the percentage of women significantly decreases in age groups older than 35 (Delano, 2003; Tsui & Lee, 2012). Newsroom policies aimed at creating a healthy work-life balance are often insufficient (Everbach, 2009). This is related to a dominant neoliberal discourse in newsrooms which emphasises individual responsibility, performance and competition. This discourse frames the decisions of women who leave the profession when they have children as a personal life choice without embedding it in a broader structural context (Kanagasabai, 2016; North, 2009).

This gendered obstacle has a connection to horizontal segregation. Hard news is associated with a need for immediate publication which imposes a demand for total availability, making working on these beats challenging to combine with caring responsibilities (Tuchman, 1973; North, 2016b). In some cases, female journalists with children prefer to work in media sectors that have more structured and regular work hours, such as magazines and radio, contrary to newspapers and news agencies. It would, however, be an oversimplification to contribute horizontal segregation entirely to a choice that is made by individual female journalists. Stereotypical assumptions and expectations also play a role in this process.

Gender expectations

Gender expectations or associations around men/masculinity and women/femininity are embedded into newsroom culture. Löfgren-Nilson (2010) draws on Gherardi (1994) when stating that this refers to how gender is 'thought' of in an organisation because it has to do with the ideas and beliefs of people. Gender expectations that are produced by gender stereotypes generate expectations about how men and women are and how they should behave (Heilman, 2001). These expectations are based on binary thinking about the skills, preferences, and abilities of men and women. These "multiple dichotomies and dualisms have served to justify women's taken for granted lesser status, including the public/private divide and the concepts of reason/emotion, mind/body and subject/object" (Bachmann et al., 2018, p. 4).

These gender binaries are problematic because they are both hierarchical and normative. Skills that are associated with masculinity are typically considered more valuable and have more status than skills that are associated with femininity. Journalists, as well as scholars, commonly express biologically essentialist viewpoints that associate men and masculinity to one side of the pair and women and femininity to the other side (North, 2016a; Lobo, Silveirinha, Torres da Silva, & Subtil, 2015). This results in a gender bias that influences evaluations in work settings and supports gender segregation.

News stories are often allocated based on expectations about differences in topic preferences, interests and writing styles between male and female journalists. The underlying assumption is that men and women produce a different kind of journalism. Van Zoonen (1998) indicated that both male and female journalists use essentialist explanatory frames and stereotypical self-images to express beliefs that women are more suited or more interested in writing soft news and better at understanding the female reader. In line with this, journalism produced by female journalists is often labelled explicitly as feminine journalism, whereas masculine journalism is considered the norm, and not labelled as such. This accentuates the otherness of female journalists (Melin, 2014).

This dichotomised gender logic of journalism reflects the gendered division between the public and private in the social order (Steiner, 2007). Hard news is commonly linked to the role of journalism to be a watchdog of democracy and provide citizens with the necessary information to participate in a rational debate in the public sphere, whereas soft news is associated more with emotions and issues that are related to the private sphere and domesticity (North, 2016b). According to Neveu (2008), this is part of a circular process through which power is constructed and gendered in the newsroom. Because women are overrepresented in soft news reporting with a more narrative writing style and a bigger emphasis on empathy and emotions, it is assumed that this writing style is an expression of feminine sensibilities. As a result, the gender division of news beats is accepted and unquestioned in journalism, even by female journalists who are pushed toward low-status topics. This reasoning is also turned upside down and linked to vertical segregation: because women have less access to leadership positions, they have fewer opportunities to develop a social network and have difficulties and problems accessing work on hard news beats.

In addition, characteristics and skills that are stereotypically associated with masculinity – such as competitiveness, decisiveness, rationality and independence – are perceived as good leadership qualities, whereas traits that are stereotypically associated with femininity – such as empathy, sensitiveness, passiveness and emotionality – are considered bad leadership qualities (North, 2016a). Scholars conclude that this results in a glass ceiling that limits the opportunities of women to make it to decision-making positions (Robinson, 2008). The metaphor of the glass ceiling is, however, criticised by others because it invokes the idea that there is only one obstacle that women have to overcome at one single moment in their career (Franks, 2013).

Interaction

Informal networks also play a role in limiting the opportunities of women to decision-making positions and hard news beats (North, 2016a). Often those positions are allocated according to social bonds formed with other people at the highest echelons of the media company; predominantly men. These exclusively male networks are labelled as old boys' networks. They function as an exclusion mechanism for women in several ways (Cho & Davenport, 2007; Phalen, 2000). It is an essential channel for professional socialisation and information exchange, which means that women do not have access to the same professional information and key learning situations. The old boys' network is an example of how gender differences are reproduced through interactions in newsrooms and how expectations influence interaction and behaviour in the newsroom. In other words, how the 'gender we think' informs the 'gender we do' (Gherardi, 1994).

Furthermore, in interaction, women in journalism are frequently confronted with overt and subtle forms of sexism and sexual harassment. Studies in different national contexts show that harassment is a structural problem that is deeply rooted in the communicative style of the newsroom culture. North (2009), for example, considers it to be an expression of hegemonic masculinity and sees it as "a (repeated) practice that creates gendered journalists, in its male initiated challenge/assault, in how it makes women feel, in how they respond and in how they are understood by others" (p. 92). It is present, but remains invisible, which results in the perception that it is not a severe issue (Walsh-Childers, Chance, & Herzog, 1996). The majority of female journalists who experience harassment do not report it, sometimes because they fear reprisal (Cho & Davenport, 2007) or because the complaint is ignored (North, 2016c). As a result, women accept sexual harassment as part of the job, minimise their experiences and see it as their individual responsibility to deal with the consequences (Claringbould, Knoppers, & Elling, 2004; Hardin & Shain, 2005; Steiner, 2009). However, it has a negative impact on their career and can lead to turnover, lowered self-esteem, decreased job satisfaction and additional stress and psychological pressure, which can increase the risk of burnout.

Hacking journalism studies

Journalism studies scholars have addressed the changing context of media industries which received less attention in feminist media studies. The rise of digital technologies and the consequences for media markets and journalism have been high on the research agenda in this field. Scholarly literature has focused on how transitions such as globalisation, commercialisation and digitalisation have changed the way news is produced, distributed and consumed (Cawley, 2019; Fenton, 2010; McChesney, 2004). This has offered insight into fundamental changes that created challenges for news companies, journalists and journalism scholars (Franklin, 2014). The concept of digital disruption is frequently used to accentuate how digitalisation drastically shuffled the cards in the global media game (Bell & Taylor, 2017; Brock, 2013; Lewis, 2012; Ternes, Peterlin, & Reinardy, 2018). Other authors speak of a digital revolution to stress the radical nature and substantial magnitude of changes brought about by technological innovation (Luengo, 2014; Starkey, 2017; Ward, 2014).

From a purely technical point of view, digital content has the advantage that it can easily be exchanged between different platforms. At the macro-level, the transformation of analogue media into digital signals based on a binary code of zeros and ones created possibilities for media convergence (Garcia-Avilés & Carvajal, 2008). As a result, lines that were previously drawn between media outlets started to become less clearly defined (Deuze, 2007). Digitalisation did not only amplify the convergence of existing media outlets but also led to the emergence of new digital media platforms such as websites, blogs and social media (Saltzis & Dickinson, 2007). Traditional news organisations started to offer more content online but also faced competition from digital native players for which online was an essential component in their DNA from the outset.

This suggests that examining technological innovation does not tell the entire story of convergence. There is an essential economic aspect to it (Nielsen, 2016). Corporate interests, to a great extent, set the rhythm of these processes (Compton, 2009). Exchanging content between different channels and exploring new opportunities in news production and delivery is part of a strategy of media companies to maximise profits in difficult economic circumstances (Paulussen, 2016). The traditional business model of news media based on paid content as an indicator of attention that could be sold to advertisers was challenged by new digital-native companies (Witschge & Nygren, 2009). Online, the news is offered for free and specific audiences could be targeted by advertising, which formed a threat to sales as well as advertising revenues. In 2007, the global economic recession increased financial insecurity in the media industry (Franklin, 2014). In a context of decreased print newspaper circulation, audience and advertising revenue, mergers and takeovers reduce production and labour costs, expand negotiating power with advertisers, and create possibilities for synergy and cross-promotion (Marshall, 2008). This resulted in a trend of increased conglomeration and the consolidation of power in a smaller number of large-scale companies.

Publishers and broadcasters transformed into multimedia companies and expected journalists to move in the same direction (Deuze & Witschge, 2018). Budget cuts and the massive layoffs of journalists went hand-in-hand with higher demands to work for multiple platforms. Ample studies highlight that journalists need to produce more content in less time and with fewer resources (Boczkowski, 2004; Schudson, 2008; Singer, 2004). Deuze and Marjoribanks (2009) draw attention to this issue when they state that "the demands of the market-place (for news and news labour) can be, or are expected to be, met by reporters and editors if they perform a more flexible, adaptive, multi-skilled, mixed or even 'liquid' occupational role and professional identity" (p. 557). In the digital era, multi-skilling has become an important journalistic asset. However, journalists not only need to combine previously defined competencies with meeting the demands of different media outlets but also develop new skills to survive and thrive in the digital era (Bradshaw & Rohumaa, 2013).

Digital tools

In increasingly digitised newsrooms, journalists have access to a wide range of digital platforms to gather and disseminate information. Tools such as social media, live streaming and mobile devices can be used to contact sources, check factual details, deliver and break the news (Hermida, 2010; Pavlik, 2001; Westlund, 2013). Besides all this, they offer possibilities to journalists to increase their professional status and social capital by interacting with the public and peers, engaging in personal branding and building credibility (Hedman & Djerf-Piere, 2013; Lasorsa, 2012; Olausson, 2018; Simon, 2019).

However, the assets of new tools are not automatically accessible to all journalists. To enjoy their professional advantages, journalists must develop specific digital skills, which requires additional time investment and training. With this in mind, several authors stress the importance of journalists' agency in innovation processes (Hermida & Thurman, 2008; Marjoribanks, 2000; Paulussen & Ugille, 2008; Spyridou, Matsiola, Veglis, Kalliris, & Dimoulas, 2013). This research moves beyond solely looking at structural factors and offers insights into how journalists give meaning to changing processes and how they are applied in their daily practices. The underlying assumption here is that technology in newsrooms is culturally and socially determined. Ample studies have explored factors that stimulate or hinder the adoption of technology in newsrooms from this angle (Boczkowski, 2004; Garrison, 2001; Maier, 2000) – for example, the importance of the lack of the necessary training (Singer, 2004) and the role of the management (Krumsvik, 2008). Other authors have looked at whether differences in the speed of adoption of technology are related to socio-demographic factors (Hedman & Djerf-Piere, 2013; Hermans, Vergeer, & Pleijter, 2009).

Technologically-driven forms of journalism

Technology not only contributed to changes in journalistic practices but also generated new genres of journalism. A new area of scholarship in journalism studies focuses on forms of journalism that are emerging at the intersection of journalism and technology. Although in the literature, various labels are used such as technologically specific work (Powers, 2012), computational journalism (Anderson, 2013; Flew, Spurgeon, Daniel, & Swift, 2012; Karlsen & Stavelin, 2014), interactive journalism (Usher, 2016), data journalism (Appelgren & Nygren, 2014; Fink & Anderson, 2015) and subtle differences in definitions can be found, Coddington (2015) positions all as part of an overarching 'quantitative turn' in journalism and an increased focus on numerical information and big data. Several factors have contributed to this quantitative shift in journalism (Splendore et al., 2016). For journalists facing an abundance of digital information, computer techniques are useful to collect, process, analyse and visualise large data sets (Stavelin, 2013). For news companies involved in an intense struggle for audience attention, forms of data visualisation can offer creative and exclusive information and be a way to distinguish themselves from competitors.

As a result of these changes, skills that are primarily associated with the technology field such as programming, development and design are in demand in journalism. The integration of tech skills in journalism works in two directions. Programmers are increasingly hired in newsrooms to provide digital skills, and journalists are becoming more familiar with programming and coding (Hermida & Young, 2017); new labels, such as journo-coder, programmer-journalist, hacker-journalist and journo-programmer have been introduced. Digital skills play an essential role in how news people who work in technologically specific areas of journalism identify themselves and differentiate themselves from traditional journalists.

This interaction has also resulted in exchanges in cultural values between journalism and programming. Usher (2016) highlights that the increased prominence and importance of hackers, code and data has introduced new ways of thinking in newsrooms. Values that are characteristic of programming culture such as experimenting, innovating and problem-solving have gained ground in journalism and inspire new innovative ways of storytelling. Other research "maps the infrastructures and arenas that enable the connection between computer scientists and journalists" (Fink & Anderson, p. 468). One of those areas is data journalism, which will be discussed further in Chapter 3.

Connecting the dots

In the previous section, feminist media scholars draw attention to the need to look at news production from a gender perspective and show how specific rules and values in journalism that appear to be value-free are, in fact, gendered. However, in journalism studies overlooking gender aspects is more common place than exceptional. Ever since White (1950) studied the gatekeeping behaviour of Mr. Gates and Gieber (1964) concluded that "news is what newspapermen make it" (p. 172), studies have presented an image of a typical journalist who is male. If gender is taken into account, it is commonly approached as an unproblematic, biological variable (Robinson, 2008). For example, sociological profile studies of journalists offer valuable insights into the male-female ratio in newsrooms and allow comparisons across time and between countries but do not say anything about how gender operates as a structuring variable in the social and professional life of journalists. This gender blindness continues in recent research on technological innovation. Differences in the adoption of technologies in newsrooms are mostly linked to age in the sense that older journalists are believed to be more hesitant than their younger colleagues. Although gender discrepancies are sometimes observed, the underlying mechanisms are not explored in depth (Appelgren & Nygren, 2014; Royal, 2012).

I believe this interface is exactly where insights from feminist media scholars and journalism studies can enrich each other. The former provides the conceptual tools to look at gender processes while the latter adds an essential layer of contextual background. In particular, I found a common ground between views of journalism scholars and feminist media scholars that have the ambition to go beyond determinism. Just like gender cannot be reduced to biological characteristics, it is not possible to reduce changes in journalism to technology (Fenton, 2010; Steensen, 2009). The approach to technological innovation as a social construction which is guided by journalists' interactions, expectations, culture and identity creates a window for the inclusion of a perspective that looks at the role of gender in this process. By combing ideas from journalism studies and feminist media studies, a more comprehensive picture of new gendered challenges and opportunities in journalism can be gained. The missing link to build a bridge between those two fields of inquiry is found in feminist technology studies.

Feminist technology studies

In feminist technology studies, the gendered dimensions of technology have long been highlighted, and different aspects of the gender and technology relationship have been explored. When looking at the development of this field, there are several parallels with feminist media studies. In the early days, research was characterised by a similar focus on 'women' and 'access'. Studies mainly focused on women's absence in the technology industry or, in other words, on the body count (Cockburn, 1983; Moore, Griffiths, Richardson, & Adam, 2008).

The underrepresentation of women in the ICT workforce is still confirmed in recent research, which also shows that there has been little progress over the years. For example, a study of the European Commission (2018) indicates that only 17% of ICT specialists in the European Union are women. Contrary to journalism education, where women, on average, make up the majority of students, female students are still strongly underrepresented in ICT education. Only one out of ten ICT graduates in the EU are women, and those numbers have decreased. A UNESCO report (2017) finds that globally, women represent only 35% of all students in science, technology, engineering and mathematics (STEM)-related study fields in higher education. The lowest representation was found in studies related to information, communication and technology, engineering, manufacturing and construction, and natural science, mathematics and statistics. These data illustrate that in terms of 'body count', the ICT industry performs even worse than the media industry.

These discrepancies were defined as a gendered digital divide separating men who have access to new forms of information technology from women who do not (Halford & Savage, 2010). This concept is criticised because it proposes a dichotomised structure dividing men and women into homogenous groups of haves and have-nots. Feminist technology scholars have recognised that there is more to it than a single gender gap based on a binary logic and have moved beyond issues of access to explore the relationship between gender and technology. Early debates were polarised between "profound pessimism about the inherent masculinity of ICTs among the early research in contrast to unwarranted optimism about the liberating potential of ICTs for women among the recent research" (Wajcman, 2007, p. 287). In the last decades of the twentieth century, a subtler analysis gained ground that leaves room both for positive and negative aspects. This social constructivist perspective starts from the assumption that gender and technology are mutually shaped or coproduced (Faulkner, 2001; Hackett, Amsterdamska, Lynch, & Wajcman, 2007; Lie, 2003).

Mutual shaping

Inspired by the work of Judith Butler (1990), research increasingly started drawing on the notions of performativity or doing gender that see gender and technology as socially shaped together instead of looking at gender as a fixed attribute that is isolated and independent from technology (Wajcman, 2010). Just like in feminist media research, this went hand-in-hand with a shift in framing of concerns in terms of 'gender' rather than 'women'. Scholars have, for example, explored how gender and technology are socially constructed in society and contribute to the underrepresentation of women in ICT education and professions (Faulkner, 2001; Henwood, 2000). These insights are particularly useful in light of increased interaction between journalism and the technology field.

Feminist technology researchers highlight that gender expectations play an essential role in limiting the opportunities of women in technology, which might sound familiar from discussions in feminist media studies. Indeed, gender expectations on technology skills work in a very similar way as the ones sustaining gender segregation in journalism. Studies show that ICT skills are gendered based on the stereotype that men are 'naturally' more technologically competent than women (Faulkner, 2001; Henwood, 2000; Moore et al., 2008). Kelan (2007) shows that people working in ICT companies take subject positions that confirm or challenge the traditional gender binary. Several female participants in her study were 'doing gender' by distancing themselves from technology because they considered it 'masculine', whereas other women were 'doing gender differently' and crossing gender boundaries by openly expressing their passion for computers. In the same line of thinking, Henwood (2000) found that women often take a subject position in which they underestimate their competence. This lack of confidence in women toward the use of technology was confirmed in other research (Herring, Ogan, Ahuja, & Robinson, 2006; McDonald & Spencer, 2000; Meraz, 2008; Peterson, 2010).

Geek stereotypes

Moreover, studies have indicated that terms such as 'hacking', 'coding' or 'programming' are far from gender-neutral. As early as 1984, Sherry Turkle pointed out that computer programming is socially constructed as a male domain through a connection with hacker culture. In her study of how colleagues and students at the Massachusetts Institute of Technology (MIT) looked at computing, she found that "the image of 'the computer person' was constructed around a very special community within the computer-science world known as 'computer hackers,' elsewhere called 'computer wizards,' 'computer wheels,' 'computer freaks,' or 'computer addicts'" (Turkle, 2005, p. 186). Later in her book, Turkle sheds light on a gender dimension in this construction when she explains that "though hackers would deny that theirs is a macho culture, the preoccupation with winning and of subjecting oneself to increasingly violent tests make their world peculiarly male in spirit, peculiarly unfriendly to women" (p. 216). This image is also evoked by metaphors of competition, sports and violence. According to Turkle, this association of computer programming with hacker culture and, on top of that, of hacker culture with male nerd masculinity is one of the reasons why women cannot identify with the area.

More recent studies have picked up on this idea and indicate that stereotypes portraying computer scientists as being nerdy, anti-social and obsessed with computers play an essential role in the underrepresentation of women in the technology field (Corneliussen, 2014; Rasmussen & Håpnes, 1991). Margolis and Fisher's study (2002) of computer science students shows that even though this 'geek mythology' is not an accurate image of people working in computer programming, it has particular gender consequences.

Women were more likely to conclude that they do not belong in computer science because they do not have the same relationship to the computer and assumed that they do not have the same level of knowledge as their male peers. Many male students did not fit this stereotypical nerd image, but they did not question their ability or doubted whether computer science is the right place for them. The nerd image is a deterrent for female students to enter the field of computer science and build a career in it.

These insights should ring a bell about the importance of a gender perspective when terms such as 'hacker', 'programmer', 'code' and 'data' are becoming more and more common in journalists' job titles, advertisements, and discourse. These categorisations are not neutral but can contain gendered assumptions and associations that can lead to gender bias and create privileges and disadvantages related to technological innovation in journalism. Feminist technology studies provide theoretical and methodological tools to analyse technology and gender simultaneously in equal depth. It is the last piece of the puzzle to study how gender, journalism and technology are socially constructed and co-produced.

References

Acker, J. (1990). Hierarchies, jobs, bodies: A theory of gendered organizations. *Gender & Society*, *4*(2), 139–158.

Acker, J. (1992). Gendering organizational theory. In A. Mills & P. Tancred (Eds.), *Gendering organizational analysis* (pp. 248–260). Thousand Oaks, CA: Sage.

Aldridge, M. (2001). The paradigm contingent career? Women in regional newspaper journalism. *Sociological Research Online*, *6*(3). Retrieved from www.socresonline.org.uk/6/3/aldridge

Anderson, C. W. (2013). Towards a sociology of computational and algorithmic journalism. *New Media & Society*, *15*(7), 1005–1021.

Appelgren, E., & Nygren, G. (2014). Data journalism in Sweden: Introducing new methods and genres of journalism into 'old' organizations'. *Digital Journalism*, *2*(3), 394–405.

Bachmann, I., Harp, D., & Loke, J. (2018). Through a feminist kaleidoscope: Critiquing media, power, and gender inequalities. In D. Harp, J. Loke, & I. Bachmann (Eds.), *Feminist approaches to media theory and research* (pp. 1–15). Cham, Switzerland: Palgrave Macmillan.

Bell, E., & Taylor, O. (2017). *The platform press: How Silicon Valley reengineered journalism*. Retrieved from http://towcenter.org/wp-content/uploads/2017/04/The_Platform_Press_Tow_Report_2017.pdf

Boczkowski, P. (2004). *Digitizing the news: Innovation in online newspapers*. Cambridge, MA: MIT Press.

Bradshaw, P., & Rohumaa, L. (2013). *The online journalism handbook: Skills to survive and thrive in the digital age*. London, UK and New York, NY: Routledge.

Brock, G. (2013). *Out of print: Journalism and the business of news in the digital age*. London, UK: Kogan Page.

Bulkeley, C. C. (2004). Whose news? Progress and status of women in newspapers (mostly) and television news. In R. R. Rush, C. E. Oukrop, & P. J. Creedon (Eds.), *Seeking equity for women in journalism and mass communication education: A 30-year update* (pp. 183–204). London, UK and Mahwah, NJ: Lawrence Erlbaum.

Burks, K. K., & Stone, V. A. (1993). Career-related characteristics of male and female news directors. *Journalism Quarterly*, *70*(3), 542–549.

Butler, J. (1990). *Gender trouble: Feminism and the subversion of identity*. London, UK: Routledge.

Byerly, C. M. (2004). Women and the concentration of media ownership. In R. R. Rush, C. E. Oukrop, & P. J. Creedon (Eds.), *Seeking equity for women in journalism and mass communication education: A 30-year update* (pp. 245–262). London, UK and Mahwah, NJ: Lawrence Erlbaum.

Byerly, C. M. (2011). *The global report on the status of women in news media*. Washington, DC: International Women's Media Foundation.

Byerly, C. M. (2013). *The Palgrave international handbook of women in journalism*. New York, NY: Palgrave Macmillan.

Byerly, C. M. (2018). Feminism, theory, and communication: Progress, debates, and challenges ahead. In D. Harp, J. Loke, & I. Bachmann (Eds.), *Feminist approaches to media theory and research* (pp. 19–35). Cham, Switzerland: Palgrave Macmillan.

Cawley, A. (2019). Digital transitions: The evolving corporate frameworks of legacy newspaper publishers, *Journalism Studies*, *20*(7), 1028–1049. doi:10.1080/1461670X.2018.1481348

Chambers, D., & Steiner, L. (2010). The changing status of women journalists. In S. Allan (Ed.), *The Routledge companion to news and journalism studies* (pp. 49–59). New York, NY: Routledge.

Cho, S., & Davenport, L. D. (2007). Gender discrimination in Korean newsrooms. *Asian Journal of Communication*, *17*(3), 286–300.

Christmas, L. (2008). Women in the media in the UK. Progress at a snail's pace. In R. Fröhlich & S. Lafky (Eds.), *Women journalists in the Western world: What surveys tell us* (pp. 123–138). Cresskill, NJ: Hampton Press.

Claringbould, I., Knoppers, A., & Elling, A. (2004). Exclusionary practices in sport journalism. *Sex Roles*, *51*(11–12), 709–718.

Cockburn, C. (1983). Caught in the wheels. *Marxism Today*, *27*, 16–20.

Coddington, M. (2015). Clarifying journalism's quantitative turn. A typology for evaluating data journalism, computational journalism, and computer-assisted reporting. *Digital Journalism*, *3*(3), 331–348.

Compton, J. R. (2009). Newspapers, labor and the flux of economic uncertainty. In S. Allan (Ed.), *The Routledge companion to news and journalism studies* (pp. 591–601). New York, NY: Routledge.

Corneliussen, H. G. (2014). Making the invisible become visible: Recognizing women's relationship with technology. *International Journal of Gender, Science and Technology*, *6*(2), 209–222.

de Bruin, M. (1999). Gender, media production and media output. *Media Development, 56*(2), 50–54.

de Bruin, M. (2000). Gender, organizational and professional identities in journalism. *Journalism, 1*(2), 217–238.

Delano, A. (2003). Women journalists: What's the difference? *Journalism Studies, 4*(2), 273–286.

Demoor, M., Saeys, F., De Bleeckere, N., Reymenants, G., & De Clercq, M. (2000). *Gezocht: M/V in het nieuws: De invloed van gender als productievariabele op de vrouw- en manbeelden in de media.* Diepenbeek, Belgium: Limburgs Universitair Centrum.

Deuze, M. (2007). *Media work.* Cambridge, UK and Malden, MA: Polity Press.

Deuze, M., & Marjoribanks, T. (2009). Newswork. *Journalism, 10*(5), 555–561.

Deuze, M., & Witschge, T. (2018). Beyond journalism: Theorizing the transformation of journalism. *Journalism, 19*(2), 165–181.

Diekerhof, E., Acker, H., Elias, M., & Sax, M. (1986). *Voor zover plaats aan de perstafel: vrouwen in de dagbladjournalistiek, vroeger en nu.* Amsterdam, the Netherlands: Meulenhoff Informatief.

EIGE (2013). *Review of the implementation of the Beijing platform for action in the EU member states: Women and the media – Advancing gender equality in decision-making in media organisations.* Luxembourg, LU: Publications Office of the European Union.

Elmore, C. (2007). Recollections in hindsight from women who left: The gendered newsroom culture. *Women and Language, 3*(2), 18–27.

European Commission. (1991). *Equal opportunities in European broadcasting: A guide to good practice.* Brussels, Belgium: European Commission.

European Commission. (1999). *Images of women in the media: Report on existing research in the European Union.* Brussels, Belgium: European Commission.

European Commission. (2018). *Women in the digital age.* Retrieved from http://ec.europa.eu/newsroom/dae/document.cfm?doc_id=50224

Everbach, T. (2009). Family-friendly? A study of work-life balance in journalism. *Media Report to Women, 37*(2), 12–18.

Everbach, T., & Flournoy, C. (2007). Women leave journalism for better pay, work conditions. *Newspaper Research Journal, 28*(3), 52–62.

Faulkner, W. (2001). The technology question in feminism: A view from feminist technology studies. *Women's Studies International Forum, 24*(1), 79–95.

Fenton, N. (2010). News in the digital age. In S. Allan (Ed.), *The Routledge companion to news and journalism studies* (pp. 557–567). New York, NY: Routledge.

Fink, K., & Anderson, C. W. (2015). Data journalism in the United States: Beyond the "usual suspects". *Journalism Studies, 16*(4), 467–481.

Flew, T., Spurgeon, C., Daniel, A., & Swift, A. (2012). The promise of computational journalism. *Journalism Practice, 6*(2), 157–171.

Franklin, B. (2014). The future of journalism: In an age of digital media and economic uncertainty. *Digital Journalism, 2*(3), 254–272.

Franks, S. (2013). *Women and journalism.* London, UK and New York, NY: I.B. Tauris & Co.

Fröhlich, R., & Lafky, S. A. (2008). *Women journalists in the Western world*. Cresskill, NJ: Hampton Press.

Gallagher, M. (1981). *Unequal opportunities: The case of women and the media*. Paris, France: UNESCO.

Gallagher, M. (1982). Negotiation and control in media organizations and occupations. In M. Gurevitch, T. Bennet, J. Curran, & J. Woolacott (Eds.), *Culture, society and the media* (pp. 151–173). London, UK: Methuen.

Gallagher, M. (1984). *Employment and positive action for women in the television organizations of the EEC member states*. Brussels, Belgium: European Commission.

Gallagher, M. (1987). *Women and media decision-making. The invisible barriers*. Paris, France: UNESCO.

Gallagher, M. (1995a). *An unfinished story: Gender patterns in media employment*. Paris, France: UNESCO.

Gallagher, M. (1995b). *Employment patterns in European broadcasting: Prospects for equality in the 1990s*. Brussels, Belgium: European Commission.

Gallagher, M. (2001). The push and pull of action research in feminist media studies. *Feminist Media Studies*, *1*(1), 11–15.

Garcia-Avilés, J. A., & Carvajal, M. (2008). Integrated and cross-media newsroom convergence: Two models of multimedia news production – The cases of Novetécnica and La Verdad Multimedia in Spain. *Convergence*, *14*(2), 221–239.

Garrison, B. (2001). Diffusion of online information technologies in newspaper newsrooms. *Journalism*, *2*(2), 221–239.

Gherardi, S. (1994). The gender we think, the gender we do in our everyday organizational lives. *Human Relations*, *47*(6), 591–610.

Gieber, W. (1964). News is what newspapermen make it. In L. A. Dexter & D. A. White (Eds.), *People, society and mass communications* (pp. 172–182). New York, NY: Free Press.

GMMP. (1995). *Global Media Monitoring Project: Women's participation in the news*. London, UK: World Association for Christian Communication.

GMMP. (2000). *Who makes the news? Global Media Monitoring Project*. London, UK: World Association for Christian Communication.

GMMP. (2005). *Who makes the news? Global Media Monitoring Project*. London, UK: World Association for Christian Communication.

GMMP. (2010). *Who makes the news? Global Media Monitoring Project*. London, UK: World Association for Christian Communication.

GMMP. (2015). *Who makes the news? Global Media Monitoring Project*. London, UK: World Association for Christian Communication.

Hackett, E. J., Amsterdamska, O., Lynch, M. E., & Wajcman, J. (2007). *The handbook of science and technology studies* (3rd ed.). Cambridge, MA: MIT Press.

Halford, S., & Savage, M. (2010). Reconceptualizing digital social inequality. *Information, Communication & Society*, *13*(7), 937–955.

Hardin, M., & Shain, S. (2005). Strength in numbers? The experiences and attitudes of women in sports media careers. *Journalism and Mass Communication Quarterly*, *82*(4), 804–819.

Hardin, M., Shain, S., & Poniatowski, K. (2008). There's no sex attached to your occupation: The revolving door for young women in sports journalism. *Women in Sports & Physical Activity Journal*, *17*(1), 68–79.

Hedman, U., & Djerf-Piere, M. (2013). The social journalist: Embracing the social media life or creating a new digital divide. *Digital Journalism*, *1*(3), 368–385.

Heilman, M. E. (2001). Description and prescription: How gender stereotypes prevent women's ascent up the organizational ladder. *Journal of Social Issues*, *57*(4), 657–674.

Hemlinger, M. A. (2001). *Women in newspapers: How much progress has been made?* Evanston, IL: Northwestern University Media Management Center.

Hemlinger, M. A., & Linton, C. C., & Smith, M. P. (2002). *Women in newspapers: Still fighting an uphill battle*. Evanston, IL: Northwestern University Media Management Center.

Henwood, F. (2000). From the woman question in technology to the technology question in feminism: Rethinking gender equality in IT education. *European Journal of Women's Studies*, *7*(2), 209–227.

Hermans, L., Vergeer, M., & Pleijter, A. (2009). Internet adoption in the newsroom: Journalists' use of the internet explained by attitudes and perceived functions. *Communications*, *34*(1), 55–71.

Hermida, A. (2010). Twittering the news: The emergence of the ambient journalism. *Journalism Practice*, *4*(3), 297–308.

Hermida, A., & Thurman, N. (2008). A clash of cultures: The integration of user-generated content within professional journalistic frameworks at British newspaper websites. *Journalism Practice*, *2*(3), 343–356.

Hermida, A., & Young, M. L. (2017). Finding the data unicorn: A hierarchy of hybridity in data and computational journalism. *Digital Journalism*, *5*(2), 159–176.

Herring, S. C., Ogan, C., Ahuja, M., & Robinson, J. C. (2006). Gender and the culture of computing in applied IT education. In E. Trauth (Ed.), *Encyclopaedia of gender and information technology* (pp. 474–481). Hershey, PA: Information Science Publishing.

Hochschild, A. (1997). *The time bind: When work becomes home and home becomes work*. New York, NY: Metropolitan Books.

Hollings, J., Lealand, G., Samson, A., & Tilley, E. (2007). The big NZ journalism survey: Underpaid, under-trained, under-resourced, unsure about the future – But still idealistic. *Pacific Journalism Review*, *13*(2), 175–197.

Holman, K. (1992). *Women in the news: International survey of women's rights in journalism*. Brussels, Belgium: International Federation of Journalists.

Holman, K., & Ortiz, S. (1992). *Equal opportunities for short term contract and freelance workers in broadcasting*. Brussels, Belgium: European Commission.

Kanagasabai, N. (2016). In the silences of a newsroom: Age, generation, and sexism in the Indian television newsroom. *Feminist Media Studies*, *16*(4), 663–677.

Karlsen, J., & Stavelin, E. (2014). Computational journalism in Norwegian newsrooms. *Journalism Practice*, *8*(1), 34–48.

Kelan, E. K. (2007). Tools and toys: Communicating gendered positions towards technology. *Information, Communication & Society*, *10*(3), 358–383.

Kim, K. (2006). Obstacles to success of female journalists in Korea. *Media Culture & Society*, *28*(1), 123–141.

Krumsvik, A. H. (2008, April). *The role of journalists in a digital age: Strategy and structure for online news production case studies of CNN and NRK*. Paper presented at the 9th International Symposium on Online Journalism, Austin, TX.

Lasorsa, D. (2012). Transparency and other journalistic norms on Twitter. *Journalism Studies*, *13*(3), 402–417.

Lewis, S. C. (2012). From journalism to information: The transformation of the knight foundation and news innovation. *Mass Communication and Society*, *15*(3), 309–334.

Lie, M. (2003). *He, She and IT revisited: New perspectives on gender in the information society*. Oslo, Norway: Gyldendal Akademisk.

Lobo, P., Silveirinha, M. J., Torres da Silva, M. T., & Subtil, F. (2015). In journalism, we are all men: Material voices in the production of gender meanings. *Journalism Studies*, *18*(9), 1148–1166.

Löfgren-Nilsson, M. (2010). 'Thinkings' and 'doings' of gender: Gendering processes in Swedish television news production. *Journalism Practice*, *4*(1), 1–16.

Luengo, M. (2014). Constructing the crisis of journalism: Towards a cultural understanding of the economic collapse of newspapers during the digital revolution. *Journalism Studies*, *15*(5), 576–585.

Lünenborg, M. (1997). *Journalistinnen in Europa: Eine international vergleichende Analyse zum Gendering im sozialen System Journalismus*. Opladen, Germany: Westdeutscher Verlag.

Maier, S. (2000). Digital diffusion in newsrooms: The uneven advance of computer-assisted reporting. *Newspaper Research Journal*, *21*(2), 95–110.

Margolis, J., & Fisher, A. (2002). *Unlocking the clubhouse: Women in computing*. London, UK and Cambridge, MA: The MIT Press.

Marjoribanks, T. (2000). *News corporation, technology and the workplace*. Singapore: Green Giant Press.

Marshall, T. (2008). *The changing newsroom: What is being gained and what is being lost in America's daily newspapers?* Washington, DC: Pew Research Center Project for Excellence in Journalism.

McChesney, R. W. (2004). *The problem of the media*. New York, NY: Monthly Review Books.

McDonald, S., & Spencer, L. (2000). Gender differences in web navigation: Strategies, efficiency, and confidence. In E. Balka & R. K. Smith (Eds.), *Women, work, and computerization: Charting a course to the future* (pp. 174–181). Boston, MA: Kluwer Academic Publishers.

Melin, M. (2014). Flight as fight re-negotiating the work of journalism. In C. Fuchs & M. Sandaval (Eds.), *Critique, social media and the information society* (pp. 231–247). New York, NY: Routledge.

Meraz, S. (2008). Women and technology: How socialization created a gender gap. In P. Pointdexter, S. Meraz, & A. Schmitz Weiss (Eds.), *Women, men, and news: Divided and disconnected in the news media landscape* (pp. 99–116). Oxon, UK and New York, NY: Routledge.

Moore, K., Griffiths, M., Richardson, H., & Adam, A. (2008). Gendered futures? Women, the ICT workplace and stories of the future. *Gender, Work & Organization*, *15*(5), 523–542.

Neveu, E. (2008). Women journalists, gendered genres and the renewal of the French press. In R. Fröhlich & S. Lafky (Eds.), *Women journalists in the Western world: What surveys tell us* (pp. 157–178). Cresskill, NJ: Hampton Press.

Nicholson, J. O. (2007). Women in newspaper journalism (since the 1990s). In P. J. Creedon & J. Cramer (Eds.), *Women in mass communication* (3rd ed., pp. 35–46). Thousand Oaks, CA: Sage.

Nielsen, R. K. (2016). The business of news. In T. Witschge, C. W. Anderson, D. Domingo, & A. Hermida (Eds.), *The SAGE handbook of digital journalism* (pp. 51–67). Los Angeles, CA: Sage.

North, L. (2009). *The gendered newsroom: How journalists experience the changing world of media*. Cresskill, NJ: Hampton Press.

North, L. (2012). Women's struggle for top jobs in the news media. In R. Francis, P. Grimshaw, & A. Standish (Eds.), *Seizing the initiative: Australian women leaders in politics, workplaces and communities* (pp. 262–270). Melbourne, Australia: eSholarship Research Centre of the University of Melbourne.

North, L. (2016a). Still a 'blokes club': The motherhood dilemma in journalism. *Journalism*, *17*(3), 315–330.

North, L. (2016b). The gender of "soft" and "hard" news. Female journalists' views on gendered story allocations. *Journalism Studies*, *17*(3), 356–373.

North, L. (2016c). Damaging and daunting: Female journalists' experiences of sexual harassment in the newsroom. *Feminist Media Studies*, *16*(6), 495–510.

Olausson, U. (2018). The celebrified journalist: Journalistic self-promotion and branding in celebrity constructions on Twitter. *Journalism Studies*, *19*(16), 2379–2399.

Paulussen, S. (2016). Innovation in the news. In T. Witschge, C. W. Anderson, D. Domingo, & A. Hermida (Eds.), *The SAGE handbook of digital journalism* (pp. 192–206). Los Angeles, CA: Sage.

Paulussen, S., & Ugille, P. (2008). User-generated content in the newsroom: Professional and organisational constraints on participatory journalism. *Westminster Papers in Communication and Culture*, *5*(2), 24–41.

Pavlik, J. V. (2001). *Journalism and new media*. New York, NY: Columbia University Press.

Peterson, H. (2010). The gendered construction of technical self-confidence: Women's negotiated positions in male-dominated, technical work settings. *International Journal of Gender, Science and Technology*, *1*(2), 66–88.

Phalen, P. F. (2000). Pioneers, girlfriends and wives: An agenda for research on women and the organizational culture of broadcasting. *Journal of Broadcasting & Electronic Media*, *44*(2), 230–247.

Pointdexter, P., & Harp, D. (2008). The softer side of news. In P. Pointdexter, S. Meraz, & A. Schmitz Weiss (Eds.), *Women, men, and news: Divided and disconnected in the news media landscape* (pp. 85–96). Oxon, UK and New York, NY: Routledge.

Powers, M. (2012). In forms that are familiar and yet-to-be-invented: American journalism and the discourse of technologically specific work. *Journal of Communication Inquiry*, *36*(24), 24–43.

Rasmussen, B., & Håpnes, T. (1991). Excluding women from the technologies of the future? A case study of the culture of computer science. *Futures*, *23*(10), 1107–1119.

Reinardy, S. (2009). Female journalists more likely to leave newspapers. *Newspaper Research Journal*, *30*(3), 42–57.

Robinson, G. J. (2005). *Gender, journalism, and equity: Canadian, U.S., and European perspectives*. Cresskill, NJ: Hampton Press.

Robinson, G. J. (2008). Theorizing the impact of gender in Canadian journalism. In R. Fröhlich & S. Lafky (Eds.), *Women journalists in the Western world: What surveys tell us* (pp. 27–48). Cresskill, NJ: Hampton Press.

Ross, K. (2001). Women at work: Journalism as en-gendered practice. *Journalism Studies*, *2*(4), 531–544.

Ross, K. (2014). Women in media industries in Europe: What's wrong with this picture? *Feminist Media Studies*, *14*(2), 326–330.

Ross, K., & Carter, C. (2011). Women and news: A long and winding road. *Media, Culture & Society*, *33*(8), 1148–1165.

Royal, C. (2012). The Journalist as programmer: A case study of the New York times interactive news technology department. *#ISOJ: The Official Research Journal of the International Symposium for Online Journalism*, *2*(1), 5–24.

Saltzis, K., & Dickinson, R. (2007). Inside the changing newsroom: Journalists' responses to media convergence. *Aslib Proceedings: New Information Perspectives*, *60*(3), 216–228.

Schudson, M. (2008). *Why democracies need an unlovable press*. Cambridge, UK and Malden, MA: Polity Press.

Simon, F. M. (2019). What determines a journalist's popularity on Twitter? *Journalism Studies*, *20*(8), 1200–1220.

Singer, J. B. (2004). Strange bedfellows? The diffusion of convergence in four news organizations. *Journalism Studies*, *5*(1), 3–18.

Splendore, S., Di Salvo, P., Eberwein, T., Groenhart, H., Kus, M., & Porlezza, C. (2016). Educational strategies in data journalism: A comparative study of six European countries. *Journalism*, *71*(1), 138–152.

Spyridou, L. P., Matsiola, M., Veglis, A., Kalliris, G., & Dimoulas, C. (2013). Journalism in a state of flux: Journalists as agents of technology innovation and emerging news practices. *International Communication Gazette*, *75*(1), 76–98.

Starkey, G. (2017). The new kids on the block: The pictures, text, time-shifted audio, and podcasts of digital radio journalism online. In B. Franklin & S. A. Eldridge (Eds.), *The Routledge companion to digital journalism* (pp. 469–477). New York, NY: Routledge.

Stavelin, E. (2013). *Computational journalism: When journalism meets programming* (Unpublished doctoral dissertation), University of Bergen, Bergen, Norway.

Steensen, S. (2009). What's stopping them? Towards a grounded theory of innovation in online journalism. *Journalism Studies*, *10*(6), 821–836.

Steiner, L. (2007). Sexed and gendered bodies in journalism textbooks. In P. J. Creedon & J. Cramer (Eds.), *Women in mass communication* (3rd ed., pp. 9–22). London, UK: Sage Publications Inc.

Steiner, L. (2009). Gender in the newsroom. In K. Wahl-Jorgensen & T. Hanitzsch (Eds.), *The handbook of journalism studies* (pp. 116–129). New York, NY: Routledge.

Stone, V. (2000). *Race, gender, and TV news careers*. Retrieved from www.missouri.edu/iourvs/tvracemf.html

Ternes, B., Peterlin, L. J., & Reinardy, S. (2018). Newsroom workers' job satisfaction contingent on position and adaptation to digital disruption. *Journalism Practice*, *12*(4), 497–508.

Tsui, C. Y. S., & Lee, F. L. F. (2012). Trajectories of women journalists' career in Hong Kong. *Journalism Studies*, *13*(3), 370–385.

Tuchman, G. (1973). Making news by doing work: Routinizing the unexpected. *American Journal of Sociology*, *79*(1), 110–131.

Tuchman, G. (1978). *Making news: A study in the construction of reality*. New York, NY: Free Press.

Turkle, S. (2005). *The second self. Computers and the human spirit. Twentieth anniversary edition*. Cambridge, MA & London, UK: The MIT Press.

UNESCO. (2017). *Cracking the code: Girls' and women's education in science, technology, engineering and mathematics (STEM)*. Retrieved from https://unesdoc.unesco.org/ark:/48223/pf0000253479

Usher, N. (2016). *Interactive journalism: Hackers, data, and code*. Urbana, IL: University of Illinois Press.

van Zoonen, L. (1994). *Feminist media studies*. Thousand Oaks, CA: Sage Publications.

van Zoonen, L. (1998). A professional, unreliable, heroic marionette: M/F: Structure, agency and subjectivity in contemporary journalism. *European Journal of Communication*, *1*(1), 123–143.

Wajcman, J. (2007). From women and technology to gendered technoscience. *Information, Communication & Society*, *10*(3), 287–298.

Wajcman, J. (2010). Feminist theories of technology. *Cambridge Journal of Economics*, *34*(1), 143–152.

Walsh-Childers, K., Chance, J., & Herzog, K. (1996). Sexual harassment of women journalists. *Journalism & Mass Communication Quarterly*, *73*(3), 559–581.

Ward, S. J. A. (2014). Ethics for a global digital world. *Digital Journalism*, *2*(4), 455–471.

West, C., & Zimmerman, D. H. (1987). Doing gender. *Gender & Society*, *1*(2), 125–151.

Westlund, O. (2013). Mobile news: A review and model of journalism in an age of mobile media. *Digital Journalism*, *1*(1), 6–26.

White, D. M. (1950). The 'gatekeeper': A case study in the selection of news. *Journalism Quarterly*, *27*(4), 383–390.

Witschge, T., & Nygren, G. (2009). Journalism: A profession under pressure? *Journal of Media Business Studies*, *6*(1), 37–59.

WMC. (2019). *The status of women in the U.S. media 2017*. New York, NY: Women's Media Center.

2 Is journalism gender e-qual?

This chapter explores the gender aspects of technological innovation in journalism. More specifically, it will focus on how the value of digital skills is constructed in journalism and how this relates to gender issues. What happens, for example, when news companies hire more people with a background in ICT, a field which is notorious for its gender imbalance? And is there, besides a horizontal and vertical gender divide in positions and news beats, also a new digital gender divide emerging in newsrooms? From the introduction, we know that numbers never tell the whole story. In order to gain a complete picture of gender dimensions, I not only focus on quantitative aspects but also ask more complex questions about how gender interacts with technology in journalism. The answers to these questions go further than merely describing gender divides by offering insights into underlying mechanisms supporting them.

The research reported here draws on qualitative interviews with a wide ranging sample of 37 journalism professionals between 23 and 64 years old and including 25 women and 12 men. The majority held the position of journalist or editor, while some were in middle and senior management. They worked for newspapers, magazines, online platforms, broadcasters, and international journalists' organisations such as ICIJ and Journalismfund.eu. Their digital competence levels ranged from basic spreadsheet skills to more advanced programming skills. Interviews revealed insights into how participants give meaning to technological changes in their profession and construct their experiences, attitudes, and perceptions toward gender and technology. This method is widely used in feminist research because it gives marginalised groups the chance to share their perspectives and stories in their own words (DeVault & Gross, 2006).

The results are interpreted through the lens of Bourdieu's field theory and its appropriations by feminist researchers. There is a focus on ICT skills, knowledge and competences in journalism, which are defined as digital capital; on the value, evaluation and accumulation of this kind of capital; the intersection with gender capital; and the opportunities of male and female journalists in the profession. Parts of this chapter are based on insights that were previously published in Digital Journalism (De Vuyst & Raeymaeckers, 2019, volume 7, issue 5).

The value of digital capital in journalism

The interviews began with a discussion of how news people define digital skills and evaluate the importance of having these skills in their profession. In general, interviewees believed that each journalist ought to have a basic level of digital expertise to be able to operate within the current media landscape. Experience with computers, social media, photo and video editing and data visualisation were considered essential for future journalists. Journalists who displayed a primary level of digital skills, as well as those with a more advanced level of skill attainment, agreed on this point. The audience played a central role in their motivations for gathering digital competences. Digital skills were considered necessary to unlock possibilities for multiplatform storytelling and to enable journalists to attract a broader range of news users by using better techniques. In other words, for most interviewees, digital tools represent a means to an end, which is choosing the best platform for telling a specific story to a particular audience. This focus is not so surprising considering that digital media made the preferences of audiences more quantified and visible for journalists through metrics, web analytics and feedback on social media.

Although there was a consensus among the interviewees on the importance of technology in their profession, not all digital skills were assessed equally. The value of digital capital was discursively constructed along two dimensions: namely, volume and composition. Regarding the first dimension, value expands in line with the amount of a journalist's digital capital. There was a belief that the more digital expertise journalists gather, the more they will be able to translate their skills into recruitment and career opportunities. On the second dimension, the value depends on how the digital capital of a journalist is internally composed as well as on its external relations with other types of accumulated capital. Internally, skills that are associated with the technology field – such as programming, coding and development – were deemed more advanced and valued higher than social media skills. Knowledge of programming languages, such as JavaScript, HTML and Python, was considered a valuable resource. A 23-year-old male magazine web editor categorised these competencies as 'hard skills'. Those advanced digital skills are associated with high levels of symbolic capital.

Contrary to basic digital skills, there were different viewpoints on who should and should not have more advanced skills. Several interviewees believed every journalist would benefit from learning to code, whereas others mentioned it depends on the type of work and the position and could be a task that is outsourced to technologists. However, despite these differences, participants agreed that by obtaining these skills, journalists can increase their status in the profession and distinguish themselves from colleagues. This went hand-in-hand with the impression that news companies are actively searching for journalists with advanced levels of digital capital. It was interesting to note that a discourse of scarcity was often part of those discussions. The pool of journalists who have these skills was considered still very limited. And as demand exceeds supply, digital expertise is perceived as an important asset for recruitment and career development. A 36-year-old male freelance journalist summarised the situation in this way:

> If you have these digital skills, it is quite easy to get a job in a job market that is very depressed at the moment. There are a lot of lay-offs, and some media are closing. Even in this context, you could still get a job quite easily. . . . I get calls from different newsrooms, sometimes twice a month, to ask whether I know someone that has these skills.

Not only how digital capital is internally composed but also its position in the full package of a journalists' capital is taken into account. Many interviewees noted that traditional journalistic skills such as writing, newsgathering, and interview skills are still fundamental, and saw digital skills as an essential add-on to the toolbox of journalists. As such, those who can combine high amounts of advanced digital capital with high quantities of traditional forms of cultural capital in journalism were placed at the top of the ranking. Since the perception is that this mix of skills seldom exists in a single person, journalism professionals who can combine both were labelled as 'unicorns'. The mythical aura surrounding unicorns emphasises the rarity and the extraordinary value of digital skills in journalism.

The word 'unicorn' also frequently appears at journalism conferences, in resources aimed at journalists, and academic publications. In their paper titled 'Finding the Data Unicorn', Alfred Hermida and Mary Lynn Young (2017), interviewed 17 data journalists in Canada and several of them made a connection between the collaborative nature of data journalism and the small number of journalists working with data. Meeting another data journalist was even described as "finding another unicorn in the middle of woods" (p. 9). A report written by Mark Stencel and Kim Perry for the Tow-Knight Center for Entrepreneurial Journalism (2016) based on a survey and interviews with 39 decision-makers at 31 news companies in the United States continued the saga and concluded that the news industry is looking for 'heroes' or 'journalists with superpowers'. The superpower being the ability to combine basic reporting, writing and editing skills with more specialised coding, audience development, visual storytelling, digital design and social media distribution skills. The superhero metaphor can be seen as another example of how digital capital is valued through a discourse of exceptionality. As we will see in the next paragraphs, this also tells something about who will meet the requirements of these positions and who will not. Just think about who usually plays the role of the superhero in movies or books.

The intersection of gender and digital capital

Finding digital capital

In predictions about journalism jobs in the future and job advertisements, terms such as code, data and algorithms increasingly feature (Future Today Institute, 2019; Royal, 2012; Wenger & Owens, 2012). New labels such as 'coder-journalist', 'hacker-journalist', 'programmer-journalist' and 'data journalist' have been created to describe these job profiles (Betancourt, 2009; Boyer, 2012; Gynnild, 2014; Usher, 2016). And just like there are different opinions among interviewees about who should have technical skills, subtle differences in these job titles carry different assumptions about the kind of know-how that is valued first and who should bring it to the newsroom. Is it a programmer who ventured into journalism and developed traditional journalism skills, a journalist who learned coding skills, or a team in which journalists work together with technologists?

Although classifying different forms of data-oriented news work can be helpful for researchers who want to compare them on several axes, in reality, the boundaries of these practices tend to be vague, and different labels are used interchangeably (Coddington, 2015). Nevertheless, what connects all the categorisations is that they signify an increased interaction and blurring of the boundaries between journalism and the technology field (Mair & Keeble, 2014). It is in this convergence of journalism and technology that gender comes into play.

Digital skills in journalism are often sought outside the media industry (Hermida & Young, 2017; Lewis & Usher, 2014). News companies have attracted people with a background in the ICT education and professions to work in technical positions such as designers, developers or programmers (Parasie & Dagiral, 2013). The ICT field is notorious for its gender imbalance, both in the professions and education. So quantitatively speaking, when more people are hired from this field, the underrepresentation of women in ICT can be replicated in journalism, where the growth in the percentage of women is fragile and stalling in recent years. During interviews, both male and female journalists noted an absence of women in technical positions in journalism, especially in programming, coding and development. Most female interviewees who work in those positions were the only women in the team. Even though journalists were not always aware of this imbalance on the job, the invisibility of women became very obvious during conferences or seminars on innovation-related themes, where women are not only underrepresented among the participants but also among the speakers.

When asked about the reasons for this underrepresentation, interviewees commonly situated this gender issue outside of journalism and saw it as a logical result of the absence of women in the technology field. For several managers, this way of thinking was based on their personal experience of difficulties in finding female applicants for tech jobs. Three women who were leading data teams could not find female candidates to fill these positions in their units. Two of them specifically wanted to hire a woman to counter the gender imbalance, but could not convince women to participate in a job interview. Since there is a tiny pool of people from ICT who want to work in journalism and an even smaller amount of women, they felt like they were looking for a needle in a haystack.

These dynamics will need to be monitored, but of course, it is not as simple as that. Even though in terms of digital technology, it is common to express things in binary codes of zeros and ones, in terms of gender, speaking in dichotomies is quite problematic. We have to move beyond simply counting men and women, and beyond the essentialist, binary thinking this often results in. Let's take it one step further and find out where these stereotypes come from, how they operate and sustain gender inequality in journalism.

Data ninjas and technical cowboys

It is necessary to make a side note to the positioning of gender imbalances in journalism and tech as a problem on the 'supply-side' in the technology labour market. Gender bias can be integrated at an early stage of the selection process, even before candidates are recruited. Language in job advertisements can contain wording that is biased toward male candidates and discourages women from applying (Bohnet, 2016).

When taking a closer look at job postings for technical positions in journalism with this point in mind, it is not difficult to find forms of gendered language. In a job posting for a data reporter, *Reuters* was looking for "a data ninja who can hunt and slay data, resulting in stories that uncover business secrets, drive markets and challenge titans of industry". The Public

Service Broadcaster of Flanders in Belgium had a position for a system engineer for radio who is a “technical cowboy”. *Mother Jones* wanted a data journalist “who is a hardcore data nerd to illuminate some of today’s most complex and urgent stories, from disinformation to corruption and financial conflicts of interest”. The *Atlanta Journal-Constitution* had a position for an experienced data journalist who is “the perfect nerd, one who combines technical, statistical and reporting sensibilities to help shape our most impactful journalism”.

For words such as ninja, wizard and cowboy, it is quite apparent that they are not gender-neutral and commonly more associated with masculinity than with femininity. Even more so, they correspond with what Connell (2005) refers to as hegemonic masculinity or the culturally idealised form of masculinity that is valued over other types that are subordinated and marginalised in society and justifies the dominant position of men over women. It is generally expressed through characteristics of ambition, strength, self-reliance, power, aggressiveness and the ability to use interpersonal violence in conflicts. Connell (1987) explains how heroes in movies, sagas, westerns, ballads or television fiction have the function of naturalising hegemonic masculinity. It is interesting to keep this in mind when looking at the hero-like status that is ascribed to journalists that combine traditional skills with digital skills. The focus on “exemplary individuals” (p. 249) or individual geniuses who are referred to as ninjas, rockstars, cowboys or unicorns creates an aura of magic around this type of work and the perception that it can only be conducted by people with unique and exceptional capabilities, which can be a deterrent for those who cannot identify with these labels to apply for jobs or build a career in journalism and tech.

The gendered nature of the word ‘nerd’ might be less obvious, but from the previous chapter, we know that it is nonetheless present. Since nerds are stereotypically portrayed as men who are anti-social, highly intelligent and utterly devoted to technology, it can be difficult for women to identify with this label and can lead to doubts about whether they belong in the field of technology and journalism. The relationship of nerd identity with hegemonic masculinity, however, is more ambiguous and complex than for the heroes discussed above. Connell (1995) positions the ‘nerd’ or ‘geek’ as a form of subordinated masculinity and sees them as part of the group of heterosexual men who are not considered as ‘real men’ because they have a lack of sports ability, physical strength, and are usually not successful in sexual relationships with women. However, the nerd stereotype incorporates aspects of hegemonic masculinity as well such as heterosexuality, intellect, rational thought and mastering technology and a lack of ‘feminine’ social and relational skills (Kendall, 2000). This type of masculinity seems very different from the ‘blokey’ or ‘macho’ masculinity that is described in previous research as hegemonic in journalism and essential in shaping newsroom culture, although the expectation that nerds are coding 24/7 does have some resemblance to the requirement of the around-the-clock availability in journalism, both of which are particularly damaging for women. Does this mean expressions of masculinity are transforming in journalism?

Definitions of hegemonic masculinity are flexible and open to change, so it is necessary to reflect on issues of power and dominance in these discussions. If technological expertise is becoming increasingly important in how power and status are defined in journalism, aspects of the previously marginalised nerd identity can become integrated into hegemonic masculinity and serve to maintain the status quo. Connell (1995) notes that even if not many men meet the definition of hegemonic masculinity, they do not challenge it because they enjoy a patriarchal dividend or an advantage from their privileged position. So even if male journalists do not comply with the image of a nerd who sacrifices his entire life to computers, their privilege to technology is still confirmed because it excludes women and other men who do not fit this image. The next part of this chapter goes deeper into the experiences of journalists with nerd stereotypes and gender issues in journalism.

The evaluation of digital capital

When discussing possible reasons for gender imbalances in technology and journalism, the interviews offered insights into how the digital skills of men and women are evaluated. Several interviewees expressed the belief that women are, in general, less tech-savvy than men and consequently also less active in tech areas of journalism. However, opinions differed on whether this should be seen as a 'software' or a 'hardware' problem. The participants who positioned this as a hardware issue evaluated digital skills based on a biological essentialist framework, in which women were presented as 'naturally' hard-wired to be less tech-savvy than men. For example, a 30-year-old male producer working for a public service broadcaster said:

> I believe women are more programmed to have a safe nest and do not take a lot of risks because of this, especially in certain phases of their life. . . . Boys experiment more by nature and dare to fall more on their face.

Although in this essentialist discourse, skills that were 'naturally' ascribed to women – such as bringing a more emotional side to stories and delivering a more human perspective – were not considered inferior to capabilities that are attributed to men, but rather as complementary; when taking into consideration how the value of digital capital is socially constructed, this gender labelling can limit the professional opportunities of women and contribute to a gendered logic associating masculinity with 'hard skills' that are highly valued in journalism.

The interviewees who saw the lack of women in tech more as a software problem referred to differences in socialisation and gender stereotypes about digital expertise. Several female interviewees gave examples of experiences before they started working in journalism of not being expected to be as technologically skilled as male peers by parents, in education and the media. For example, a 27-year-old female data journalist had experienced that, contrary to her male friends, she was not stimulated to pursue her interest in coding in school. A 64-year-old female participant working for an international journalists' organisation compared herself to her twin brother, who was encouraged to study maths and science by her parents, whereas she was stimulated to study literature. She only discovered her mathematical skills later in her career and decided to become a business journalist.

These societal stereotypes sneak into journalism and are manifested by a subtle bias toward the digital expertise of women, similar to the ICT sector (Bray, 2007; Bury, 2011; Valgaeren, 2001; Youngs, 2005). There were evident gendered differences in the experience of bias related to digital skills. While several female participants indicated that their digital expertise is always questioned or tested and that they continuously have to prove their digital skills, none of the male interviewees shared this experience. On the contrary, they were confident about their digital skills and made connections with their career advancement. While male journalists took more a subject position of confidence toward technology, it was common for female participants to express feelings of insecurity about technological innovation and describe their position in terms of 'fear' and 'distance'.

> My perception is that women were aware of the potential of technology, but they were afraid of it because it was something that they didn't understand very much and they would just let men do it.
>
> (32-year-old female interactive and animation director)

> The distance to these topics seems to be bigger than just for the male colleagues and then sometimes it seems to be too big.
>
> (32-year-old female online data journalist)

> The thing about technology is that it scares you a lot at first. Especially, obviously, when you have to make money with it. Because I've always

> been a tech-savvy person, ever since I was really young, I've always known my way around it, but having to make money out of it means knowing how to do it professionally.
>
> (30-year-old female broadcast journalist)

For example, a 30-year-old female journalist who was taking her first steps in data journalism described this feeling when she first started working for a visual journalism team of a broadcasting company: "I was incredibly scared. I actually came back home crying every day for a month because I thought that I don't know what I'm doing. This is huge!" At first, she explained her insecurity about her technical skills based on the lack of statistical training in her journalism education. Later in the interview, when discussing opportunities for male and female journalists, she looked at this from a gender perspective:

> I think we as women are very afraid of what we think we can do. And we think we can't do many things because we've been taught for a long time that we couldn't do many things. That we had no aptitude to do many things. So I think we are very afraid of asserting ourselves. And I say this from personal experience.

Furthermore, several interviewees saw this as one of the reasons why female journalists are being less vocal about their skills or less inclined to apply for technical positions when they do not meet all the listed criteria in the job advertisement. A 46-year-old female freelance journalist had the feeling that if women were more involved in self-promotion, they would be invited to more conferences on digital innovation and be able to share their ideas with the public. Three other female participants mentioned that when decisions for recruitment or promotions are made, they would be hesitant to talk openly about their digital expertise, whereas their male counterparts would exaggerate their skills:

> I always have the feeling that I am incompetent and that I don't know anything. And then I compare myself to all my male colleagues . . . and they just strut around and say I know this, I know that. . . . And it might be true, but I have less confidence.
>
> (33-year-old female broadcast journalist)

> I've seen many women that know a lot but don't like to brag about it. . . . It's very difficult to generalise, but men are more like, 'I am here, and this is my thing', right? I've seen that many men have less

> problems promoting themselves and promoting what they know than women.
>
> (31-year-old female data journalist working for an international journalists' organisation)

> Women have always been the ones who did not stand up and say: 'yes, of course, I am doing it'. Even if they are not that experienced in something. They think this is something you have to be very good at, in order to be able to do it.
>
> (32-year-old female data editor working for an online medium)

The lack of self-confidence of women toward technology is also found in other studies (Herring, Ogan, Ahuja, & Robinson, 2006; McDonald & Spencer, 2000). In line with the work of Elisabeth Kelan (2007, 2008), the subject position that some of the female journalists were taking toward technology could be interpreted as a way that women were 'doing gender' because it confirms traditional gender conceptions about digital expertise. However, at the same time, it is essential to take into account that female journalists are constantly reminded of their gender with their technical skills repeatedly being underestimated in the newsroom and in society, which can result in the belief that they are not as good in technology as male colleagues.

The coding ceiling

This gendered logic also seemed to be a reference point in how interviewees defined what a technical position is and what is not. Social media management, audience development, and product placement were often not considered 'technical positions', even though they require technical skills such as data and statistical analysis. Several participants had the impression that these positions are valued less than programming and development, which are often immediately labelled 'technical'. In this respect, it is interesting to go back to the discussion about which digital skills are considered necessary in the current media landscape and note that programming and development were mentioned much more than skills for audience development or product management. A 37-year-old female founder of a news start-up looked at this status differential through an intersectional lens:

> A truly excellent product manager who may not be a coder but can link up the editorial side of the business, the revenue side and the technology together, is incredibly valuable. Product and audience development

> are roles which we see a lot of more women going into and people of colour also, and I worry that that's why we are not recognising the importance of that work and paying it equitably. I think that it is undervalued in general in the industry.

The reflection of this interviewee is in line with explanations put forward by feminist media scholars for gender segregation in journalism. What this tells us is that although the gendered evaluation of digital skills seems like a completely new barrier, there are many parallels with the traditional gender barriers described in Chapter 1. For example, with the essentialist thinking about the writing skills of male and female journalists that sustains horizontal segregation or with the gender stereotypical ideas about the management capacities that result in the misconception that women are less competent and less suitable for leadership positions that contribute to the glass ceiling. Is the traditional glass ceiling accompanied by a coding ceiling that makes it difficult for women to build a career in programming positions? Chapter 3 will explore this question more in-depth in the context of data journalism. For now, we can conclude that gender expectations are deeply integrated into journalism culture also in new digital spaces that are developing in recent years at the junction of journalism and technology.

The accumulation of digital capital

During the interviews, participants talked about how they gathered their digital capital. First, the route of traditional journalism education was explored. Two points are essential to take into account in relation to this path. First, that many participants saw an overrepresentation of female students in traditional journalism education, but were not convinced this would be immediately translated into higher opportunities in the job market because there is too little emphasis on advanced computer skills. A 23-year-old male magazine web editor, for example, believed that journalism curricula were lagging and had yet to embrace multimedia production and digital storytelling techniques fully. Moreover, he was convinced that news companies would prefer candidates with an educational background in computer sciences rather than applicants who studied journalism. According to the web editor, this could have a negative impact on the opportunities for women in journalism because ICT education is still very male-dominated. A 49-year-old female participant working for an international journalists' organisation agreed with this point of view:

> If currently they are hiring programmers, and there is a majority of male programmers, then the women who study journalism, but don't

> know how to do the programming, just don't have the competence that the classic media are looking for right now.

Most interviewees had not attained their digital expertise in traditional education but through self-study. Trying and experimenting with new digital tools was described as a matter of trial and error. Many interviewees mentioned that possibilities for internal training in digital skills in their newsrooms are limited, but that there is a wide range of external training possibilities such as online courses (e.g., MOOCs), conferences, hackathons and evening classes. Although these forms of education were considered quite democratic because they are open and often free of charge, not all journalists have equal opportunities for access. Obtaining access required a considerable investment of time, mostly in the weekend or after working hours, which intersected with access to support for childcare. A 48-year-old female data editor at a newspaper drew a connection between work-life balance, age and the data unicorn ideal when she noted that this is only attainable for young journalists who do not have family responsibilities outside of work:

> I've watched several unicorns develop and what they did is they spent all their non-working hours teaching themselves new skills. This was before they were married, before they had kids and had all the free time in the world. I just thought: you are crazy! Yes, it can help your career, but you have just wasted some great years of your life in which you need to be having fun. Several of them are now parents, and I can see that they've stalled in their ability to learn something new and don't have time anymore to do it. I work all day, and then I go home and go to my other job of taking care of the kids.

It was clear from the interviews that this was a gendered issue considering that especially female participants mentioned work-life balance issues as an obstacle that limits training opportunities and keeping track with all technological innovations. For example, a 28-year-old female editor-in-chief of a newspaper explained how she tries to balance these different demands:

> I don't have a lot of time to play with all these new tools and bring them into the newsroom. My thing is, where am I going to take that time from? From my son? From cleaning? From cooking? From my husband? . . . For one app, I will probably need 12 hours to really learn, implement and use it. . . . And it's probably going to change again in a year or two. . . . I think the important thing is to choose right now which ones you would really need for your work and be smart about where you are going to take that time from. And the most important thing: don't feel guilty if you don't know all of the innovations.

This is another example of how new gendered obstacles emerging in this increasingly digitalised field intersect with the more traditional ones. These findings add new insights to debates on the gendered work-life balance in journalism. Whereas, in previous studies, this is mostly seen as one of the reasons why women leave journalism and have limited access to decision-making positions and social capital, these results show that the combination of the need for continually staying up to date with the latest innovations intensifies the pressure on the work-life balance and limits the access of especially women to digital capital in journalism.

Furthermore, it was not only the amount of time but also the moments that should be invested in external training that discouraged several female interviewees from participating in them. A 32-year-old female online data journalism editor shared her experience on work-life balance and participating in hackathons where data journalists and technologists can exchange knowledge and collaboratively improve their skills:

> Most hackathons are also on the weekend, for example, so you have to be really keen on working with your computer, even on Saturday and Sunday. But you won't find this type of colleague amongst women that much. At least in my experience. I don't know if I can really, I can only say this about myself. I really like this work, but I see that to be balanced I need some other things.
>
> (32-year-old female data journalist)

There is a second gender aspect related to the issue of time investment and digital skills in journalism that can be deduced from her quote. Another worry that she is expressing is that to achieve the same level of digital expertise as her male counterparts, she would need to make sacrifices in the rest of her life and spend a significant amount of leisure time on learning and improving tech skills. This discourse of total dedication was common in how female journalists described what it takes to be a good coder. These findings mimic the results of Margolis and Fisher (2002) that show that a 'geek mythology' which portrays computer programmers as entirely devoted to programming and not having a social life is one of the reasons why women distance themselves from the information technology (IT) industry.

Conclusion

The results of this study illustrate how digital capital and gender intersect in journalism. Digital capital is increasingly recognised as valuable and legitimate in journalism. It is associated with status and can be used to gain higher recruitment and career advancement opportunities. In the words of Bourdieu, who sees symbolic capital as the outcome of the conversion of other forms of capital, we could say that digital capital can be exchanged for high amounts of symbolic capital in journalism. This exchange, however, is gendered.

Even though women and men might have the same amount of digital capital, women will have more trouble translating their digital capital into symbolic capital. Their digital capital is often questioned or tested, or, in other words, it is not seen as 'legitimate' as men's digital capital. This works in line with Moi's (1999) conceptualisation of gender as a form of symbolic capital. Gender is a negative coefficient that intersects with the digital capital of women. As a consequence of their negative gender capital, women are less self-confident and vocal about their digital skills and have more difficulties translating them into career opportunities. In addition, the accumulation of digital capital in journalism is gendered. There is a gendered time issue which disadvantages women in gathering their digital capital, and this intersects with the work-life balance issue and stereotypical images about what it takes to excel in journalism and technology.

However, the study also shows that female participants do not consider themselves 'naturally' predestined to be less technically competent but recognise that gender stereotypes play a role in how their digital capital is evaluated in society and the newsrooms, which contrasts with Bourdieu's description of the acceptance of the gender status quo by women (Bourdieu, 2001). Chapter 4 elaborates on how women are questioning this gendered evaluation of their digital capital. It highlights the role of social capital in this consciousness and explains how this is a crucial intermediary asset in strategies that women use for empowerment through technology in journalism. Before that, we will have a look at the specific case of gender issues in data journalism in the next chapter.

References

Betancourt, L. (2009, December). *How programmer/journalists are changing the news*. Retrieved from https://mashable.com/2009/12/11/programmer-journalists/?europe=true

Bohnet, I. (2016). *What works: Gender equality by design*. Cambridge, MA: The Belknap Press of Harvard University Press.

Bourdieu, P. (2001). *Masculine domination*. Cambridge, UK: Polity Press.

Boyer, B. (2012, September). *Welcome to hacker journalism 101, take your seats*. Retrieved from www.niemanlab.org/2012/09/brian-boyer-welcome-to-hacker-journalism-101-take-your-seats/

Bray, F. (2007). Gender and technology. *Annual Review of Anthropology*, *36*(1), 37–53.

Bury, R. (2011). She's geeky: The performance of identity among women working in IT. *International Journal of Gender, Science and Technology*, *3*(1), 33–53.

Coddington, M. (2015). Clarifying journalism's quantitative turn: A typology for evaluating data journalism, computational journalism, and computer-assisted reporting. *Digital Journalism*, *3*(3), 331–348.

Connell, R. W. (1987). *Gender and power: Society, the person and sexual politics*. Stanford, CA: Stanford University Press.

Connell, R. W. (1995). *Masculinities*. Berkeley, CA: University of California Press.

Connell, R. W. (2005). Change among the gatekeepers: Men, masculinities, and gender equality in the global arena. *Sings*, *30*(3), 1801–1824.

DeVault, M. L., & Gross, G. (2006). Feminist interviewing: Experience, talk and knowledge. In S. N. Hesse-Biber (Ed.), *Handbook of feminist research: Theory and praxis* (pp. 173–197). London, UK: Sage.

De Vuyst, S., & Raeymaeckers, K. (2019). Is journalism gender e-qual? A study of the gendered accumulation and evaluation of digital capital in journalism. *Digital Journalism*, *7*(5), 554–570.

Future Today Institute. (2018, September). *2019 trend report for journalism, media, and technology*. Retrieved from www.dropbox.com/s/3mtwxmudyhn1cqb/FTI_Journalism_Trends_2019_Final.pdf?dl=0

Gynnild, A. (2014). Journalism innovation leads to innovation journalism: The impact of computational exploration on changing mindsets. *Journalism*, *15*(6), 713–730.

Hermida, A., & Young, M. L. (2017). Finding the data unicorn: A hierarchy of hybridity in data and computational journalism. *Digital Journalism*, *5*(2), 159–176.

Herring, S. C., Ogan, C., Ahuja, M., & Robinson, J. C. (2006). Gender and the culture of computing in applied IT education. In E. Trauth (Ed.), *Encyclopaedia of gender and information technology* (pp. 474–481). Hershey, PA: Information Science Publishing.

Kelan, E. K. (2007). Tools and toys: Communicating gendered positions towards technology. *Information, Communication & Society*, *10*(3), 358–383.

Kelan, E. K. (2008). Emotions in a rational profession: The gendering of skills in ICT work. *Gender, Work & Organization*, *15*(1), 49–71.

Kendall, L. (2000). Oh no, I'm a nerd! Hegemonic masculinity on an online forum. *Gender & Society*, *14*(2), 256–274.

Lewis, S., & Usher, N. (2014). Code, collaboration, and the future of journalism: A case study of the Hacks/Hackers global network. *Digital Journalism*, *2*(3), 383–393.

Mair, J., & Keeble, R. L. (2014). *Data journalism: Mapping the future*. Bury St Edmunds, UK: Abramis Academic Publishing.

Margolis, J., & Fisher, A. (2002). *Unlocking the clubhouse: Women in computing*. London, UK and Cambridge, MA: The MIT Press.

McDonald, S., & Spencer, L. (2000). Gender differences in web navigation: Strategies, efficiency, and confidence. In E. Balka & R. K. Smith (Eds.), *Women, work, and computerization: Charting a course to the future* (pp. 174–181). Boston, MA: Kluwer Academic Publishers.

Moi, T. (1999). *What is a woman?* Oxford, UK: Oxford University Press.

Parasie, S., & Dagiral, E. (2013). Data-driven journalism and the public good: Computer-assisted-reporters' and 'programmer-journalists' in Chicago. *New Media & Society*, *15*(6), 853–871.

Royal, C. (2012). The Journalist as programmer: A case study of the New York times interactive news technology department. *#ISOJ: The Official Research Journal of the International Symposium for Online Journalism*, *2*(1), 5–24.

Stencel, M., & Perry, K. (2016). *Superpowers: The digital skills media leaders say newsrooms need going forward*. New York, NY: Tow-Knight Center for Entrepreneurial Journalism.

Usher, N. (2016). *Interactive journalism: Hackers, data, and code*. Urbana, IL: University of Illinois Press.

Valgaeren, E. (2001). *Loopbanen van vrouwen in management en ICT. Literatuurstudie*. Diepenbeek, Belgium: LUC-SEIN.

Wenger, D. H., & Owens, L. C. (2012). Help wanted 2010: An examination of new media skills required by top U.S. news companies. *Journalism & Mass Communication Educator*, *67*(1), 9–25.

Youngs, G. (2005). Cyberspace: The new feminist frontier? In K. Ross & C. M. Byerly (Eds.), *Women and media: International perspectives* (pp. 185–208). Oxford, Carlton and Malden, MA: Blackwell Publishing.

3 Gender issues in data journalism

Data journalism is one of the new journalistic genres that emerged in a context of increased data creation and quantification. This technologically-driven form of journalism has increasingly become part of academic and professional debates. Among professionals, much of the conversation revolves around useful tools to collect, analyse and visualise data and how to strengthen required data journalism skills (Faure, 2019; Gray & Bounegru, 2018; Rogers, 2011). These skills are also the subject of academic discussions – for example, on how data journalistic competencies are taught in higher education (Splendore et al., 2016; Yarnall, Johnson, Rinne, & Ranney, 2008). Furthermore, there is research on how data journalism is implemented in newsrooms (Appelgren & Nygren, 2014; Karlsen & Stavelin, 2014; Parasie & Dagiral, 2013), who is working in it (Flew, Spurgeon, Daniel, & Swift, 2011) and how it is interacting with the technology field (Lewis & Usher, 2013, 2014; Träsel, 2015).

The roots of data journalism are traced to Computer-Assisted Reporting (CAR) and the idea of precision journalism that gained ground in newsrooms in the late 1980s and early 1990s and signified the application of social science statistical methods in journalism and the use of computers in this process (Howard, 2014; Meyer, 1973; Uskali & Kuutti, 2015). Several factors changed the context of CAR, in which the possibilities of interacting with and communicating about data were limited and contributed to the development of data journalism. This transformation was driven by an explosion of data produced in the twenty-first century (Anderson, 2011). Several countries have seen an increased openness of government data, and large data collections have become more available online.

In an increasingly data-driven society, journalists need skills to access and analyse databases to keep fulfilling their watchdog role and present massive amounts of information in a way that makes sense to the public. By doing so, they can increase accuracy and objectivity and hold powerful institutions and governments to account (Felle, 2016). In light of this important role attributed to data journalism for the future of journalism, it is essential to look at who is taking part in this field and which voices are represented. Considering that this is an area that is still in development, it is interesting to monitor gender and diversity issues and explore whether gendered structures are reproduced in this new field or whether cultures and alternative practices are being designed that foster a more inclusive news production context and news output.

A field in development

There have been multiple attempts to define what the core of data journalism is and to differentiate it from other forms of technologically-specific styles of news work such as data-driven journalism, computational journalism, programmer-journalism and hacker-journalism (Coddington, 2015; Powers, 2012; Usher, 2016). Despite the lack of agreement on a definition, a common thread that runs through different descriptions is a reference to hybridity and convergence between several fields, more specifically between journalism and technology (Appelgren, 2018; Bell, 2012; Bradshaw, 2010; Hermida & Young, 2019). Making typologies and clarifying different forms of data-oriented news work from a top-down perspective is complicated because there tends to be overlap and exchanges between genres (Coddington, 2015). Moreover, ambiguity about the meaning of data journalism is not limited to the academic community. Qualitative research has indicated that professionals have different perspectives on the core elements of data journalism (Borges-Rey, 2016; Fink & Anderson, 2015).

This ambiguity is not necessarily an obstacle but may present opportunities. A bottom-up perspective encourages researchers to be open to the full range of "what people are doing and how they categorise what they are doing" without predefining their actions in categories (Couldry, 2004, as cited in Baack, 2018, p. 3). Fink and Anderson (2015), for example, in in-depth interviews, saw the benefit of the vagueness and contestability and decided to let journalists themselves define what 'data journalism' means to them and how they practice it. De Maeyer, Libert, Domingo, Heinderyckx, and Le Cam (2015) followed a similar approach to data journalism as a socio-discursive practice that is "shaped by the discursive efforts of all actors that are involved in it, inside newsrooms and outside newsrooms" (p. 432) to shed light on the rise of data journalism in the French-speaking part of Belgium. A study of Cheruiyot, Baack, and Ferrer-Conill (2019) focused on how actors at the periphery of the journalistic field in European and African contexts such as non-profits and civic technologists shape the practice of data journalism.

This bottom-up approach fits neatly with the conceptualisation of gender as a social construction and my focus on how journalists give meaning to categorisations based on gender and sustain or challenge gender inequalities through practice and interaction. Just like gender is not written in stone, data journalism is not fixed yet, but open for negotiation and continuously shaped and reshaped by the people in the field. Inspired by feminist technology studies, I approach data journalism and gender as mutually and socially shaped. This means that I will focus on the co-creation of gender and the culture, practices and values of data journalism. Special attention will be paid to exchanges between data journalism and the technology field.

Field theory offers valuable concepts to study these inter-field relationships as well as the internal dynamics of data journalism, power dynamics and forms of capital (Anderson, 2011, 2012; Coddington, 2015; Fink & Anderson, 2015). My approach, however, differs from a traditional field analysis in several ways. First of all, as Fink and Anderson (2015) highlighted, data journalism "has not yet solidified into anything resembling a classic Bourdieuean structure with formal poles of cultural, economic, or temporal capital" (p. 468). It is approached as a 'field in development' of which the boundaries, the ways to enter it and the skills required to succeed are still being negotiated. And second, data journalism is considered as a field that goes beyond national borders, which diverges from the emphasis that Bourdieu puts on the concrete historical and geographical circumstances of fields. The underlying reason for this decision is that data journalism projects are often characterised by an international scope with themes and teams that cross borders.

Intersection with the technology field

The emergence of data journalism is positioned in a context of increased interaction between journalists and technologists inside as well as outside news organisations. Within the newsroom, data journalism can be conducted in teams that bring together journalists, designers, developers and programmers with different skill sets and backgrounds (Borges-Rey, 2016; Gynnild, 2014; Zanchelli & Crucianelli, 2013). Outside newsrooms, hackathons, conferences and international networks and communities offer spaces where journalists can collaborate and exchange ideas with technologists. For example, Lewis and Usher (2014) borrow the concept of trading zones from Galison (1997) to refer to Hack/Hackers as an informal meeting space between journalists and technologists.

Baack (2018) found similar ties between journalists and civic technologists. The lack of institutionalised engagement and a significant degree of informality and elasticity in those encounters led to the conclusion that there is not so much a fixed and well-defined field, but more a "community of practice" (p. 3) where journalists and technologists find each other in common skills, commitments and ambitions that transcend different organisational backgrounds. As we will see in the next section, these encounters can lead to exchanges of cultural values and practices and introduce new ways of thinking about journalism.

Programming culture: values of open-source and hacker communities

'Hacks' (journalists) and 'hackers' (technologists) are increasingly collaborating and finding each other in principles of hacker and open-source culture (Lewis & Usher, 2013). The word 'hacker' has already appeared several times in this book – for example, in Chapter 2, in which the rise of the hacker-journalist was discussed. While previous sections focused more on the skills that are combined in this new job profile, this chapter will offer more insight into the exchanges of values that go hand-in-hand with these interactions. Before looking at their expression in data journalism, I will first examine some of the central values in hacker and programmer culture.

Hacker culture is commonly defined by a set of moral guidelines which, when taken together, form a hacker ethic (Himanen, 2001). One of the central values of the hacker ethic is that hackers are driven by passion and have an intrinsic interest to solve programming challenges. Creativity and innovative thinking are highly valued in hacker communities. The focus is not only on the outcome but also on the process of experimenting and tinkering with technology. Rewards are derived from solving technical problems and fixing bugs in computer systems but also from going beyond personal technical capacities and demonstrating technical mastery (Coleman, 2013). There is a meritocratic dimension to this based on the belief that "hackers should be judged by their hacking, not by bogus criteria such as degrees, age, race, or position" (Levy, 2010, p. 31). Besides self-education, peer-to-peer learning is essential to how hackers develop technical skills and knowledge. In online communication platforms, hackers help each other to solve specific problems.

The principles of transparency and freedom to exchange information are essential in this process. Hackers often publish source code, so it becomes freely available to the public and can be adapted by others. It encourages the collaborative building of knowledge. Values of transparency, collaboration and participation are also central in the open-source community (Kelty, 2008). This community is committed to Open Source Software (OSS) or Free/Libre Open Source Software (FLOSS). Both hacker and open-source communities have an underlying belief that if the conditions for the free access, modification and redistribution of software are met, technology can improve societies, uphold democracies and empower citizens.

As programming has become increasingly integrated into newsrooms, the principles of this ethic are finding their way into the mind-set of journalists and introduce new values and perspectives on news work that are different from traditional journalism (Usher, 2016). Several studies have focused specifically on how the hacker ethic is articulated in communities of data journalists (Appelgren & Nygren, 2014; Träsel, 2015). For example, Baack (2018) indicates that because of overlapping and transferable technical skills and shared tools, data journalists and civic technologists form collaborative learning communities that share a spirit for thinking, continuous learning and transparency. According to Howard (2014), there is also a collective ambition to advocate for freedom of information and understand their work as a public service that holds influential people or institutions accountable and supports active and informed citizenship. In line with this, Träsel's (2015) study of a data journalism team at a Brazilian newspaper showed that data journalists identified themselves as hackers, believed that journalism can be improved by technology and had a self-taught approach to learning.

Other research focuses on how open-source principles are being integrated into journalism. Lewis and Usher (2013, p. 615) indicated how the core normative values of open-source – transparency, iteration, tinkering and participation – offer "the opportunity for technologists and journalists together to think about traditional journalism as espousing new values – not diminishing long-standing virtues, but instead providing a new framework that makes journalism more relevant in a participatory, digital culture". Studies that focus specifically on how data journalists embrace open-source ideals find a strong belief in cooperation and transparency, collaborating to build software, sharing codes, asking for audience feedback and working with databases that are freely and openly available on the Internet (Borges-Rey, 2016; Gynnild, 2014; Palomo, Teruel, & Blanco-Castilla, 2019; Weber & Rall, 2012).

Introducing the gender perspective

Although gender issues have not been addressed much in data journalism, there have been studies conducted on this topic in the neighbouring open-source and hacker communities. Feminist scholars have made several critical reflections on the egalitarian and meritocratic values of the hacker ethic. Despite the principles that everyone should have equal access and be judged based on technical capacities rather than personal characteristics, hacker and open-source communities are predominantly young, white and male

(Powell, Husinger, & Medlin, 2010), even more so than in computer science in general. On top of the obstacles that women are already experiencing in ICT areas such as gendered evaluation of skills and nerd stereotypes, there are extra hurdles particularly for open-source and hacker communities (Hollinger, 2007).

Elements of the hacker ethic that are egalitarian in theory can create a hostile environment for women when turned into practice. Levy (2010, p. 27), for example, notes that there can be a competitive element to fixing bugs in computer systems, and hacking can become "a macho contest to prove oneself so much in command of the system that one could recognize elegant shortcuts to shave off an instruction or two, or better, rethink the whole problem and devise a new algorithm". Powell et al. (2010) found another barrier in their study in the open-source community similar to the geek mythology mentioned in Chapter 1, which is the perception that it is necessary to 'dream in code' to be successful. Just like the geek myth in programming, this is not representative for most people working in the field but does suggest that to thrive people need to sacrifice other parts of their life and constantly work on improving their coding skills. Finally, researchers have made a critical note to the collaborative nature of hacker communities and online sharing of knowledge. Anonymous communication on the Internet among hackers sometimes contains misogynistic elements and creates a locker room atmosphere that is unwelcoming to women (Herring, 2003). This implies that the principle of freedom of speech that is put forward in the hacker ethic cannot be practised by everyone in an equal manner.

Adam (2005) takes it one step further and asks why hacker communities are surrounded by a rhetoric of equality in the first place. According to her, this is based on the false assumption that the Internet and communities that are related to it break with old traditions and are inherently equal and democratic. In this context, she refers to metaphors that position the Internet as a new electronic frontier or the 'Wild West' (Brail, 1996; Jordan & Taylor, 2004; Kramer & Kramarae, 1997; Ludlow, 1996), which encourages the idea that only hackers with macho characteristics can explore it. Remember the technical cowboy metaphor in a job description for a technical position in Chapter 2? Additionally, Adam (2005) scrutinises the way hackers position themselves as "a new, alternative political movement challenging the existing order with all its baggage of racism, sexism and repression" and explains that "just because a political movement challenges a non-egalitarian orthodoxy, this does not mean that it is free from the instruments of oppression itself" (p. 140). The question that remains is when principles are exchanged between data journalism, hacker communities and open-source communities, will the gendered values inherent in them also be transferred?

The next section looks at the culture and practices of data journalism from a gender perspective drawing on data from qualitative interviews with people in the field. Thirty-one participants between 23 and 49 years old with varying backgrounds in data journalism were selected (21 women, 10 men). Twenty participants defined themselves as full-time data journalists and were working in data teams in newsrooms, start-ups or international journalists' organisations. They were involved in project management, design and programming. Five participants occasionally worked on data journalism projects. Five participants were taking initial steps in developing their data journalism skills and had participated in seminars, training sessions and hackathons. One participant was teaching a data journalism course at a Belgian university. Parts of this chapter were previously published in an article in the *Journal of Applied Journalism and Media Studies* (De Vuyst, 2018, volume 7, issue 2).

The analysis will draw on concepts from Bourdieu's field theory and its appropriations by feminists to study the accumulation of capital and strategies that are used in the field of data journalism. On the one hand, there will be a focus on how data journalists' professional networks, work practices and culture are influenced by the technology field, and how this provides opportunities in journalism for going beyond gendered obstacles such as the gendered division of news beats, the old boys' network and sexism. On the other hand, I will reflect on gendered challenges in data journalism and obstacles that are limiting gender and other forms of diversity in the field.

Entrance to the field

When discussing paths to enter data journalism, most interviewees considered it a way for newcomers and young journalists to gain access to the field of journalism. This was based on the belief that it is not only a buzzword or a popular topic at journalism conferences, but that news companies are also investing in data journalism. Prominent newsrooms such as the *New York Times*, *ProPublica* and *The Guardian* were seen as examples of how data journalism teams can be implemented successfully and produce impressive data visualisations that generate significant audience interest and traffic to online platforms. Managers of data units had experienced an increase in resources, even in times of cutbacks and lay-offs in other parts of their newsroom. In some cases, this meant regular reporter jobs were replaced by data journalist jobs. Several interviewees were convinced that, even though job opportunities are scarce in the current media landscape, news organisations are still hiring data journalists. Thus, data journalism skills were an important addition to the résumé of newcomers in journalism. These skills were considered a way to distinguish oneself from the competition and get ‘a foot in the door’ of the news industry.

Coupled with this, participants associated a different career path for young journalists entering the field of data journalism compared to those entering the field of traditional journalism. While newcomers in traditional journalism usually have to start at small, local newsrooms and gradually move up the career ladder, data journalism had opened doors for internships and positions at prestigious newsrooms for several of the study participants. The responses suggest that this is related to differences in the kind of capital that is valued at entry-level positions.

In traditional journalism, social capital in the form of personal connections and knowing the right people was highly valued at the recruitment level. This had a gender dimension. Female participants in this study noted that, in their experience, the entrance to traditional journalism is guarded by an old boys’ network, an exclusively male informal network that serves as a channel for exchanging professional knowledge and information about job vacancies and promotions. The exclusion of women from this network limits their opportunities for recruitment in traditional journalism. Data journalism, however, was considered to be a new field that is still open to everyone, regardless of gender.

The interviews suggest that digital capital is more critical than social capital when recruiting employees in the field of digital journalism. Digital capital in data journalism was defined as the skills to analyse and clean large databases and present the results in an understandable way to the public. In particular, this includes spreadsheet skills, coding skills and data visualisation capabilities. Several female journalists, who had these skills but were excluded from the male-dominated networks in traditional journalism, used data journalism as a gateway to the journalism field. One of the advantages of digital capital is that it can easily be transferred from other fields to journalism, more so than social capital, which is more specifically tied to social relationships in a particular field. This is illustrated in the following quote from a 32-year-old female data journalist who was lacking a network in journalism but was able to use her data and statistical analysis skills gathered in the corporate world to start working in a data unit at a newspaper:

> The media is a closed area. If you don’t have somebody that opens the door when you are new . . . and when you know nobody, it’s complicated. But I found a way to get in. You have to be in the right place at the right moment. And I got a good moment because when I decided to turn to journalism, data journalism was a new thing. It was experimental.

Digital capital was seen as an essential marker of difference between data journalists and traditional journalists as well as among data journalists. Interviewees had the impression that many traditional journalists lack this kind of capital; therefore, they do not fully grasp the potential of data journalism. In some cases, journalists working in data teams felt that they were considered to be outsiders in the newsrooms. Data journalists saw digital capital as the most important form of capital in their field, but the ideal data journalist was often described as a 'data unicorn' that combines digital skills with traditional journalistic capital such as news judgment, interview techniques and writing skills.

An inclusive field?

Interviewed data journalists had established their own professional networks for socialising and exchanging information. These networks go beyond boundaries between geographic regions, newsrooms as well as journalism and the technology field. Connections are made at hackathons, workshops and conferences and through online platforms. The mailing list of the National Institute for Computer-Assisted Reporting (NICAR) was mentioned as an example of this. There are plenty of blogs, discussion groups and mailing lists that are used to ask questions about data analysis, solve programming problems and share information about job vacancies and training possibilities. These networks were considered more accessible to all journalists, independent of gender, age and seniority than networks in traditional journalism. Access can be gained by a few mouse clicks, which make the threshold to enter the conversation rather low, whereas traditional journalism networks are less transparent and often segregated based on social markers. Participation in these networks allowed data journalists to increase both their digital and social capital.

In line with this, interviewees emphasised that the logic of data journalism is based more on cooperation and teamwork than traditional journalism. First, several data journalists were involved in extensive cross-border projects, such as The Migrant Files, the FarmSubsidy project, LuxLeaks and Swiss Leaks, in which journalists from different countries joined forces to analyse huge databases to expose irregularities and injustices. Second, the majority of the interviewed data journalists who work in news organisations were part of cross-disciplinary teams in which they worked together with technologists. Third, data journalist participants often shared their methods and codes online with colleagues from competing newsrooms, a practice that was linked to the open-source movement. This transparency about work methods was believed to make data journalism more inclusive.

Furthermore, several interviewees had the impression that because data journalism focuses on exposing wrongdoings in society, practitioners are more conscious about forms of discrimination and injustice in their own community. A 27-year-old female data journalist illustrated this point by mentioning a debate in the NICAR mailing list in which many members openly criticised a comment because it was considered sexist, and they demanded a code of conduct to guarantee diversity in the community and prevent harassment. This was coupled with a belief in the potential of data journalism projects to address and challenge discrimination in society and shed light on differences between communities in terms of privilege, status and opportunities. Nevertheless, several interviewees backed this up by an awareness that data can lie and biases can sneak into and distort analysis and visualisations.

Barriers to entering the field

The focus on digital skills as a decisive factor to begin and build a career in data journalism made the field of data journalism come across as egalitarian and meritocratic to several interviewees. However, not everyone shared this experience and considered their trajectory in data journalism to be one without hindrances. How data journalism is presented and represented was specifically mentioned as a barrier to enter and build a career in this field.

The focus on skills which opened doors to journalism for some served as an exclusionary mechanism for others. Several interviewees had the feeling that there are unrealistic expectations about the skills that are needed in data journalism. They gave examples of job advertisements with a long list of programming languages and journalistic skills that applicants are expected to know even when people who are working at the company cannot tick all the boxes. In line with this, labels such as 'wizard', 'ninja', 'rockstar' and 'unicorn' sustain the idea that data journalism is different from traditional journalism even though there are many similarities in terms of work practices and competences. Most interviewees could not identify with these labels. They indicated that there are very few people who combine coding and writing skills and that most data journalism work happens in a team of people with different abilities. Although the unicorn metaphor is not an accurate presentation of people working in data journalism, this kind of discourse has consequences for its inclusivity. Several female interviewees referred to this as a reason why they felt that what they needed to get their foot in the door was impossible to attain. In the following quote, a 31-year-old female data editor described her experience:

> It makes you feel like they are looking for others. Like they are looking for something that I don't have. I am not a unicorn, I am just regular

old me . . . I am no ninja or no rockstar, I know how to do X, Y and Z but I don't know if that makes me super. The way that we talk about ourselves and recruit people and look for people to work for us has to change! Otherwise, we are never going to find people that fill that diversity void, because you have that fear of . . . imposter syndrome. Where you feel like: well I am not good enough for this.

The 'geeky' part of data journalism

Even when stepping outside the mythical world of unicorns, there were implicit assumptions about who will bring particular skills to the team in data journalism connected to gender. It was noted that data journalism is sometimes split up into a coder side and a journalism side, in which men tend to work more in the former and women in the latter. The majority of the interviewed journalists indicated that women are underrepresented in technical positions in data journalism. Coding and development were sometimes called 'the geeky part' of data journalism and constructed as typically male areas. The quote below of a 49-year-old female participant described how this image can limit women's opportunities for being recruited to fill these positions in data journalism:

> If the assumption is that coders or those who are good at digital work or programming have to be young, men with a hood, eating pizza, drinking Coca-Cola, not washing for days and making dirty remarks . . . then you wouldn't imagine a woman among them unless she really changes herself.

When discussing reasons for this gender division of tasks in data journalism, several interviewees referred to a large number of people who are hired from civic tech or the open-source communities to work in technical positions in data journalism, and just like in Chapter 2, this was positioned as a consequence of the underrepresentation of women in those communities. However, several female interviewees talked about their experience of being pushed toward 'more softer areas' based on gender stereotypical assumptions about skills when working in data journalism teams, whereas men would take up the tech part. For example, this 31-year-old female data editor who worked in several data teams claimed:

> Especially when I was working on more collaborative projects, the way that things would get divided up into how we would attempt to tackle the project, is like, the guys: oh well I will do the coding part on this,

> why don't you work with the reporter on the text? Why don't you talk to the audience team about promotion? Why don't you handle the more project managy tasks and I will do the technical stuff?

Lack of diversity

Additionally, a lack of diversity in data journalism was a reason why several participants felt like they do not belong in the field. The intensity of this feeling was connected to the intersection of multiple identities that amplified experiences of not feeling represented in data journalism. When discussing gender diversity, several participants observed a significant increase of women working in data journalism in recent years and claimed that women went from being entirely absent to having proper representation in data journalism, a trend that they noticed especially at conferences. However, female data journalists still constitute a minority, and several women referred to a lack of female role models since, internationally, the data journalism community is represented by a handful of people who are mostly white men.

Even though interviewees referred to a positive trend in terms of gender diversity, they did not see a similar shift in terms of ethnic and racial diversity. The data journalism community is predominantly white. A 31-year-old female data editor described how she had to overcome hurdles related to different aspects of her identity to enter into data journalism when she talked about her experience of going to data journalism conferences:

> When you feel like there is this white wall in front of you that is impenetrable, that is really intimidating! As a young black female, I am like: I don't have the same skill level as you, I don't have the same degree as you, so why would you in this position of power want to help me who is not?

Being a black woman in a mainly white, male field resulted in the perception that she would not be accepted by the data journalism community. Later on in the interview, she described how this feeling slowly started to fade after having personal interactions with other data journalists:

> I started talking to colleagues at conferences, and pretty much everyone I talked to is willing to help, and they are welcoming. It's just getting over that initial fear that . . . the fear and the intimidation that you feel like you are going to be not welcome. It's just a perception. Once you get past that mental block that people are going to be awful or mean, it's okay. But we don't do enough with the promotion and the PR to

> make people feel comfortable enough to get past that mental block and that fear or intimidation.

In sum, these excerpts from the interviews show that *how* and by *whom* data journalism is represented can have an impact on who feels part of the community and who feels entitled to the right to take part in its values of openness and collaboration. Although data journalism is often presented as an open field, its potential for empowerment cannot be fully realised if these barriers for entrance are kept in place.

Navigating the field

Although several barriers were sustained, it was not an entirely negative story, and data journalism offered opportunities for women to build a career and avoid some of the traditional obstacles of journalism. Several interviewed women used data journalism as a way to avoid some of the gendered barriers that they are experiencing in traditional journalism. Female data journalists who had previous experience in traditional journalism were familiar with the gendered division of media sectors and news beats. Some of them were pushed to cover softer topics and features news that were associated with low symbolic capital, based on essentialist notions about their preferences and skills. They opted for a career in data journalism because it gave them more autonomy in choosing the topics they wanted to cover and increased their access to hard news beats. It allowed them to work in areas of journalism that are commonly associated with a good deal of status and are strongly guarded by the old boys' network. In the quote below, a 24-year-old female data journalist who is working for an international journalists' organisation illustrated this point with investigative journalism:

> Investigative reporting is traditionally a very male-dominated field. Most of them are in their 50s or 60s. It's a little circle of people, and it used to be very hard to get in. If you look today, there are a lot of women. And I think it's because data journalism takes the focus away from the people you know, your circle and the networking, and puts more emphasis on your skills. This gets you through a huge barrier for women, because if you know how to do it, you just have to do it, and you'll be fine. This is different from being accepted by a group of people and building relationships with sources.

In line with this, several interviewees used data journalism as a tool to address gender-related issues, women's rights and sexism – topics that are often labelled 'women's themes' and typically receive little attention in traditional media. They had developed projects on femicide, motherhood, court cases on sexual assault, violence on trans women and trends of representative female MPs. For them, data journalism was a tool to make silenced voices heard and create narratives outside of the traditional and stereotypical news frames.

Furthermore, several female participants stated that male-dominated networks go beyond the newsroom to include personal relationships between male journalists and male elite news sources, such as politicians, government officials and economists. They felt that it was harder for them to gain access to male sources than for their male colleagues. Male sources were sometimes reluctant to share information with female journalists. Several female journalists were confronted with harassment and sexism from male sources. They believed that they would have to face this obstacle less frequently in data journalism because the newsgathering in that area of journalism is primarily based on databases and spreadsheets and female journalists are less dependent on elite sources. A 30-year-old female interviewee working for a non-profit journalists' organisation was convinced that data journalism can help women avoid violent or risky situations when reporting on sensitive topics:

> A woman journalist is able to publish stories that maybe she wasn't able to cover before . . . because she doesn't have to put herself at risk to get that information. It makes it easier. One of my colleagues was covering violence . . . in a really, really dangerous region in Colombia. She got to measure killings and could put those numbers into a story because of data journalism.

Cracking the coding ceiling?

Furthermore, several participants believed that women are better represented in the decision-making positions of data teams in data journalism than in traditional journalism. Three female interviewees who were managing those data teams shared this point of view. They had access to leadership positions in data journalism that would be difficult to achieve in traditional journalism because of the glass ceiling. However, once these women had acquired these decision-making positions in data teams, they felt that their career progress was slower than male journalists in similar jobs. A female data editor had the impression that she had been given fewer opportunities to expand her activities and hire new people than the men who were leading data teams. She related this to men being more direct and assertive when negotiating with management.

Her male colleagues would, for example, threaten to leave the newsroom if they did not receive more resources for their teams. A 33-year-old female participant who is leading a data team at a public service broadcaster explained that she is the only woman around the table in meetings with decision-makers from other departments. This made it more difficult for her to join the discussion and propose ideas. The quote below illustrates how she was confronted with the old boys' network in her position:

> Even more than they had to . . . I had to fight for my stories, and I had to convince them. I had the feeling that I always had to be prepared, you know. . . . That is not the most optimal way of fitting in. It's different when you are a man, and you are part of the boys' club.

For male interviewees, gender was less of an issue during the development of a career in data journalism. A male participant who combines programming with journalism explained that he did not see gender as a problem to career-building in data journalism in the first place but had only become aware of the privilege linked to gender in building a data team when he became a mentor for a female colleague in the same position and none of his advice or suggested strategies worked for her:

> I had this moment that I realised when we were talking that all of the advice that I had given her was wrong. Because the advice I was giving her was things that I could do because I am a six-foot-tall, white guy with a beard. There is a lot of advice like: just do it! And just deal with the consequences! Just push forward! A lot of the ways that I was able to be successful at [name of newspaper], where I had to push the organisation to get shit done, they just weren't going to fly for her, because of how she was perceived.

His experience shows how privilege can be invisible to those who have it. Raising awareness of privilege and disadvantage will be essential to make power dynamics visible, challenging the gendered status quo and create data journalism where female leadership and inclusive collaborations can be developed. In the concluding part of this book, I will reflect on several ways in which this can be achieved.

Conclusion

The study's findings suggest that data journalism is constructed as a subfield of journalism with its own doxa, community and logic. There are several indications that the rules of the game are different for data journalism than for traditional journalism, which had specific gender aspects. Several elements expressed in the interviews with data journalists remind us of the hacker ethic that was described earlier in this chapter. The interviewed data journalists had a strong belief in feedback from peers, transparency and collaboration. This was one of the reasons why the community and spaces that data journalists use for exchanging social capital and professional knowledge were considered inclusive and easily accessible to both female and male journalists. Just like hackers, some of them took an activist position and believed in the potential of data journalism to expose wrongdoings in society and scrutinise structural inequalities. For several interviewees, this position was connected with feminist ambitions to raise awareness of gender issues through data journalism projects. On top of this, there was an expectation that data journalists will be judged based on their technical competences and not so much on parts of their social identity and social capital in the field. The focus on having the right digital capital made data journalism come across as meritocratic and egalitarian. It seemed to offer newcomers and young journalists the opportunity to enter the field of journalism and pursue a career.

This applied especially to female journalists who entered data journalism to bypass some of the gendered obstacles in traditional journalism. First, it allowed female journalists to avoid the old boys' network that was limiting their chances for recruitment in traditional journalism (Melin, 2008). Second, some of the women believed they would experience less harassment and sexism from sources in data journalism because they could rely more on data to write their stories. Third, female data journalists tried to go beyond the gendered dichotomy between soft–hard news beats and media sectors, which is based on essentialist assumptions in traditional journalism. In data journalism, they had access to prestigious, traditionally male-dominated news beats. Working in data journalism offered women opportunities to increase their symbolic capital in the profession.

However, this openness of data journalism has to be put into perspective since the interviews also offered insight into exclusionary mechanisms. Data journalism is not entirely free of gender-related obstacles. Positions in data journalism were socially constructed as gendered. In fact, the research participants noted that coding and development are still perceived as the geeky part of data journalism, and this geek stereotype resulted in less access for women. Forms of gender bias can sneak into collaborations in data journalism projects and sustain this gender segregation of tasks. Furthermore, the presentation of data journalism as a field for 'unicorns' resembles the dynamics of the nerd stereotype, which is connected to the assumption that a high level of skills is necessary to make it in the area. In this way, the gender inequalities of traditional journalism can be replicated in data journalism, even though this field has the ability to challenge bias in the content and in the production. The next chapter focuses on how feminist action is necessary for data journalism to reach this potential for empowerment.

References

Adam, A. (2005). *Gender, ethics, and information technology*. Hampshire, UK: Palgrave Macmillan.

Anderson, C. W. (2011). *Notes towards an analysis of computational journalism*. Berlin, Germany: Alexander von Humboldt Institut für Internet und Gesellschaft.

Anderson, C. W. (2012). Towards a sociology of computational and algorithmic journalism. *New Media & Society*, *15*(7), 1005–1021.

Appelgren, E. (2018). The illusion of interactivity: The paternalistic side of data journalism. *Journalism Practice*, *12*(3), 308–325.

Appelgren, E., & Nygren, G. (2014). Data journalism in Sweden: Introducing new methods and genres of journalism into 'old' organizations'. *Digital Journalism*, *2*(3), 394–405.

Baack, S. (2018). Practically engaged: The entanglements between data journalism and civic tech. *Digital Journalism*, *6*(6), 673–692.

Bell, E. (2012). Journalism by numbers. *Columbia Journalism Review*, *51*(3), 48–49.

Borges-Rey, E. (2016). Unravelling data journalism: A study of data journalism practice in British newsrooms. *Journalism Practice*, *10*(7), 833–843.

Bradshaw, P. (2010). *How to be a data journalist*. Retrieved from www.theguardian.com/news/datablog/2010/oct/01/data-journalism-how-to-guide

Brail, S. (1996). The price of admission: Harassment and free speech in the wild, wild west. wired_women. In L. Cherny & E. Wise (Eds.), *Gender and new realities in cyberspace* (pp. 141–157). Seattle, WA: Seal Press.

Cheruiyot, D., Baack, S., & Ferrer-Conill, R. (2019). Data journalism beyond legacy media: The case of African and European civic technology organizations. *Digital Journalism*. doi:10.1080/21670811.2019.1591166

Coddington, M. (2015). Clarifying journalism's quantitative turn: A typology for evaluating data journalism, computational journalism, and computer-assisted reporting. *Digital Journalism*, *3*(3), 331–348.

Coleman, G. E. (2013). *Coding freedom: The ethics and aesthetics of hacking*. Princeton, NJ: Princeton University Press.

De Maeyer, J., Libert, M., Domingo, D., Heinderyckx, F., & Le Cam, F. (2015). Waiting for data journalism. A qualitative assessment of the anecdotal take-up of data journalism in French-speaking Belgium. *Digital Journalism*, *3*(3), 432–446.

De Vuyst, S. (2018). Cracking the coding ceiling: Looking at gender construction in data journalism from a field theory perspective. *Journal of Applied Journalism and Media Studies*, *7*(2), 387–405.

Faure, G. (2019, September). *7 essential data journalism tools for investigative reporters*. Retrieved from https://ijnet.org/en/story/7-essential-data-journalism-tools-investigative-reporters

Felle, T. (2016). Digital watchdogs? Data reporting and the news media's traditional "fourth estate" function. *Journalism, 17*(1), 85–96.

Fink, K., & Anderson, C. W. (2015). Data journalism in the United States: Beyond the "usual suspects". *Journalism Studies, 16*(4), 467–481.

Flew, T., Spurgeon, C., Daniel, A., & Swift, A. (2011). The promise of computational journalism. *Journalism Practice, 6*(2), 157–171.

Galison, P. (1997). *Image and logic: A material culture of microphysics*. Chicago, IL: University of Chicago Press.

Gray, J., & Bounegru, L. (2018). *The data journalism handbook 2: Towards a critical data journalism practice*. Amsterdam, The Netherlands: Amsterdam University Press.

Gynnild, A. (2014). Journalism innovation leads to innovation journalism: The impact of computational exploration on changing mindsets. *Journalism, 15*(6), 713–730.

Hermida, A., & Young, M. L. (2019). *Data journalism and the regeneration of news*. Oxon, UK and New York, NY: Routledge.

Herring, S. C. (2003). Gender and power in online communication. In J. Holmes & M. Meyerhoff (Eds.), *The handbook of language and gender* (pp. 202–228). Oxford, UK: Blackwell.

Himanen, P. (2001). *The hacker ethic and the spirit of the information age*. London, UK: Vintage.

Hollinger, A. (2007). *The culture of open source computing*. Boulder, CO: National Center for Women & Information Technology.

Howard, A. B. (2014). *The art and science of data-driven journalism: When journalists combine new technology with narrative skills, they can deliver context, clarity, and a better understanding of the world around us*. New York, NY: Tow Foundation and the John S. Knight Foundation.

Jordan, T., & Taylor, P. A. (2004). *Hacktivism and cyberwars: Rebels with a cause?* London, UK and New York, NY: Routledge.

Karlsen, J., & Stavelin, E. (2014). Computational journalism in Norwegian newsrooms. *Journalism Practice, 8*(1), 34–48.

Kelty, C. M. (2008). *Two bits: The cultural significance of free software*. Durham, NC: Duke University Press.

Kramer, J., & Kramarae, C. (1997). Gendered ethics on the internet. In J. Makau & R. Arnett (Eds.), *Communication ethics in an age of diversity* (pp. 226–243). Urbana, IL: University of Illinois Press.

Levy, S. (2010). *Hackers: Heroes of the computer revolution*. Sebastopol, CA: O'Reilly.

Lewis, S., & Usher, N. (2013). Open source and journalism: Toward new frameworks for imagining news innovation. *Media, Culture & Society, 35*(5), 602–619.

Lewis, S., & Usher, N. (2014). Code, collaboration, and the future of journalism: A case study of the Hacks/Hackers global network. *Digital Journalism, 2*(3), 383–393.

Ludlow, P. (1996). *High noon on the electronic frontier: Conceptual issues in cyberspace*. Cambridge, MA and London, UK: MIT Press.

Melin, M. (2008). *Gendered journalism cultures: Strategies and tactics in the field of journalism in Britain and Sweden* (Unpublished doctoral dissertation), University of Göteborg, Göteborg, Sweden.

Meyer, P. (1973). *Precision journalism: A reporter's introduction to social science methods*. Bloomington, IN: Indiana University Press.

Palomo, B., Teruel, L., & Blanco-Castilla, E. (2019). Data journalism projects based on user-generated content. How La Nacion data transforms active audience into staff. *Digital Journalism*. doi:10.1080/21670811.2019.1626257

Parasie, S., & Dagiral, E. (2013). Data-driven journalism and the public good: Computer-assisted-reporters' and 'programmer-journalists' in Chicago. *New Media & Society*, *15*(6), 853–871.

Powell, W. E., Hunsinger, D. S., & Medlin, B. D. (2010). Gender differences within the open-source community: An exploratory study. *Journal of Information Technology Management*, *21*(4), 29–37.

Powers, M. (2012). In forms that are familiar and yet-to-be-invented: American journalism and the discourse of technologically specific work. *Journal of Communication Inquiry*, *36*(24), 24–43.

Rogers, S. (2011, July). *Data journalism at the Guardian: What it is and how we do it?* Retrieved from www.theguardian.com/news/datablog/2011/jul/28/data-journalism.

Splendore, S., Di Salvo, P., Eberwein, T., Groenhart, H., Kus, M., & Porlezza, C. (2016). Educational strategies in data journalism: A comparative study of six European countries. *Journalism*, *71*(1), 138–152.

Träsel, M. (2015, September). *Hacks and Hackers: The ethos and beliefs of a group of data-driven journalism professionals in Brazil*. Paper presented at the Future of Journalism Conference, Cardiff, UK.

Usher, N. (2016). *Interactive journalism: Hackers, data, and code*. Urbana, IL: University of Illinois Press.

Uskali, T., & Kuutti, H. (2015). Models and streams of data journalism. *The Journal of Media Innovations*, *2*(1), 77–88.

Weber, W., & Rall, H. (2012, July). *Data visualization in online journalism and its implications for the production process*. Paper presented at the 16th International Conference on Information Visualisation, Montpellier, France.

Yarnall, L., Johnson, J. T., Rinne, L., & Ranney, M. A. (2008). How post-secondary journalism educators teach advanced CAR and data analysis skills in the digital age. *Journalism & Mass Communication Educator*, *26*(2), 146–164.

Zanchelli, M., & Crucianelli, S. (2013). *Integrating data journalism into newsrooms*. Retrieved from www.icfj.org/sites/default/files/integrating%20data%20journalism-english_0.pdf.

4 Hacking the gender gap

Even though the previous chapters indicate that technological advancement comes with several gendered challenges, a dichotomisation in which digital skills are considered to belong to the 'male sphere' of journalism would be an oversimplification. Digital skills are also part of strategies aimed at the empowerment of women. This chapter will shed light on initiatives designed to hack the gender gap in journalism and technology. In these initiatives, female journalists are building digital knowledge, giving new meanings to nerd stereotypes and developing their own narratives on technology. The aim is to share knowledge about good practices and take the discussion to a theoretical level by making connections with previous research on the reproduction and challenges of the gender status quo in journalism. There will be a focus on three kinds of initiatives and feminist strategies for resistance and emancipation: community building and networks, mentoring and feminist hackathons.

Community building and networks

The consolidation of networks and mentoring relationships has already proved a form of leverage for women on the path to decision-making power but also has significant merits when it comes to gaining digital expertise. Several female interviewees have created and joined networks aimed at redefining the relationship between gender and technology. By doing so, they want to break the symbolic association between masculinity and technology and challenge gender stereotypes about technical skills. There are several initiatives, events and organisations that focus on inspiring women and girls to start and build a career in technology and computer science such as Webgrrls, Women Who Code, PyLadies, Black Girls Code and Girls Who Code. Some organisations are explicitly directed at empowering women through technology in journalism. Two examples that illustrate the power of networking in the struggle for gender equality in journalism and tech are Chicas Poderosas and WanaData.

Chicas Poderosas is a non-profit founded in 2013 by Mariana Santos during an ICFJ Knight Fellowship. This initiative started in Latin America and has grown with communities in more than ten countries, including in Europe and the United States (Chicas Poderosas, 2019). The objective is to encourage and support women to excel in digital journalism and become leading innovators in digital media. In 2015, female journalists from different countries in Latin America were invited to a 'training the trainers' event at Stanford University with workshops on improvisation and design, leadership, entrepreneurship and innovative journalism. These women became Chicas Poderosas ambassadors and brought back the knowledge to their own country where they started national or regional chapters. By organising digital and new media and leadership training, investigative journalism workshops and hackathons, Chicas Poderosas wants to provide female journalists with the tools and skills that are necessary to scrutinise structural inequalities in their countries and set up collaborative projects that address injustices that go beyond geographic borders. Besides this, female journalists from Latin America can apply for fellowships to work in digitally advanced newsrooms where they can be involved in innovative projects, expand their network and build mentoring relationships. Finally, there is a News Venture Lab, which is a 20-week accelerator for women who want to start in entrepreneurship for independent digital media.

Another initiative that is inspired by the same goal is WanaData. This network started in 2017 as the Naija Data Ladies with three chapters in Nigeria focusing on increasing gender diversity in media and technology (WanaData, 2019). The network was launched under Code for Africa, a civic media organisation that was developed by a team of ICFJ Knight Fellows with regional hubs in Kenya, Nigeria, South Africa and Tanzania. WanaData supports women in data journalism and promotes projects on different issues such as malnutrition, maternal health and human trafficking. In 2018, the network was expanded to a Pan-African scope with additional chapters in Kenya, South Africa, Tanzania and Uganda. Several in-depth reporting projects have been established through partnerships with newsrooms.

Although there is a different geographic focus, the idea behind these organisations is similar: women come together and support each other in gaining digital skills to expand their opportunities in an increasingly digitalised field of journalism. According to participants in those networks, the advantages of these initiatives are not only related to the digital training possibilities but also the positive impact and self-confidence building toward digital technology. To several interviewees, these initiatives offered a 'safe space' to experiment with digital innovations. A safe space means that they feel more comfortable to contribute to discussions and take the lead in projects because they can share ideas in a supportive environment without being confronted with gender prejudices about their skills. A 31-year-old female data journalist described her experience with safe spaces in the following way:

> The obstacles for women to work with other women would be really lower than to work with other men because most of your male colleagues have. . . . If they are really into tech, they have spent hours and hours in front of a computer, that you don't have. So it's always a bit frustrating for me to try to learn something with male colleagues because in most cases, I am really slow compared to them.

Besides increasing self-confidence about digital skills, those networks also provide a fruitful ground for creating strategies for emancipation. During the events, participants developed and strengthened their feminist awareness and openly questioned male dominance related to innovation in journalism. There is room for discussions on experiences of gendered obstacles in journalism and knowledge is shared on how to overcome them. To resist gender bias, female journalists collaborated with women in the technology field to increase their digital capital and break these stereotypes. Their homologous positions and the experience of similar gender barriers created a sense of solidarity and a spirit of emancipation among the women in these networks. This is encouraged in several hands-on workshops, for example, on leadership, understanding harassment and developing an online security strategy. The aim is to develop strategies to empower female journalists with digital skills to change gender inequality in journalism.

It is important to note that social capital plays a central part in strategies for the emancipation of female journalists. The increased self-confidence was closely related to the numerous opportunities for women to expand their social capital during these events. This social capital was constructed based on two aspects. First of all, these initiatives offer spaces to female journalists for networking and accumulating more social capital. By doing so, women can counteract their negative gender capital and oppose the old boys' network in journalism. A 32-year-old female interactive and animation director expressed this in the following quote:

> Men that are friends with men. It's like the boys' club. And then women do not feel that support and empowerment that men feel. So it's a room full of men, and of course, the woman is going to feel less empowered because the men have their friends and they feel empowered. I believe Chicas is also aimed at creating these networks of support for women so we can help and support each other. When we are in doubt, we can have a group of women where we can go and ask support and feel

> empowered, like the boys' club does. So it's kind of creating a girls' club as well.

Exchanging social capital is not limited to face-to-face interaction, but also happens through a wide range of online platforms where the networking continues in WhatsApp groups, mailing lists and on social media. Several interviewed women shared knowledge on recruitment and career opportunities with other women and felt empowered through this mutual support they received online.

Mentoring

The second aspect of the construction of social capital is mentoring, which was an essential foundation for these initiatives. In addition to increasing digital capital, these networks aim to increase social capital by cultivating and strengthening mentoring relationships among women. During the interviews, several female interviewees mentioned that having a mentor they can talk to about their insecurities and questions about technologies increased their confidence in their digital skills. Some of them referred to other women who they saw as role models and had encouraged them to start coding, enter into tech areas in journalism and aspire to decision-making positions in the field. Although female role models were rare in journalism and technology, they had a significant impact on many women in the study and inspired them to do the same for other female colleagues.

Making these role models more visible and accessible is the rationale behind Digital Women Leaders, an initiative that was started by Katie Hawkins-Gaar (DigitalWomenLeaders, 2019). It provides a digital platform that helps women in digital journalism to get in touch with possible mentors. Again, the link between mentoring, technology and decision-making power is central. The website of this initiative, digitalwomenleaders.com, features women who are graduates of either Poynter's Leadership Academy for Women in Digital Media or Online News Organization's Women's Leadership Accelerator. Both are programs that involve academies with talks, hands-on activities and discussions focused on building women's leadership and management skills. Graduates of these programs offer free one-on-one coaching sessions for other female journalists. An appointment can be made directly through the website. For every potential mentor, there is a description of the current position and on which aspects the person can provide coaching – for example, on building hands-on skills in data science, visual journalism and audience engagement or career development skills such as dealing with imposter syndrome and managing work/life balance. In doing so, the project is trying to address problems related to the underrepresentation of women in management and coupled with this the challenges that women journalists face to build network relationships. One of the mentors in the project explained why she chose to be involved:

> Network power is really, really important for promoting yourself, your career and moving up in the media industry. And what we are trying to do is build really transparent networks where it's easy for people to plug in and meet people in powerful positions who can mentor or sponsor them in some way and that whole thing has taken off.

The lack of transparency in networks has been a hurdle for women's opportunities since they entered the profession. A lot of networking happens after working hours and in informal and invisible ways which can be disadvantageous for women. Digital platforms are used to make networking more transparent and take away the threshold women face in journalism to get in touch with a mentor. Moreover, the exchange of social capital through mentoring is reciprocal. Later in the interview, this participant explained how being a mentor benefitted her career and improved the overall quality of journalism in her newsroom:

> Those sessions are also a good way for me to build my networks and recruit new people. It's not only an altruistic thing. When you are actively working on diversity, it makes your team better, your network stronger and it helps you and your business grow in the right way. I feel like I've gotten way more out of that than a lot of the women who just come in for a session. Because it allows me to go like, 'hey, I know this person who is a great data journalist, and I know you are looking for somebody, and I think you should hire them'. And that creates strong ties.

In this way, mentoring can be the missing link between digital capital and women's leadership. As we have seen earlier, digital skills are not enough to increase the opportunities for women in journalism. A female interviewee summarised this in the following statement and explained how the value of digital capital is limited when it is not backed by a considerable amount of decision-making power:

> It has to be not only about digital skills, but also about leadership skills because you can . . . understand a lot about technology, but if you are not given the room and space to mentor and to lead and to come up with ideas, then how can you be innovative? At the end of the day, it would be an industry led by men, so every time a woman would come up with an idea, they would not have the room to show and to test and

to experiment. The men in leadership would either kill the idea or try to own it.

(32-year-old female interactive and animation director)

We know from Chapter 2 that even when women have a similar or a higher level of digital skills, they often face difficulties in getting the value of those skills recognised and translate them into career opportunities. Long lists of expectations and qualifications to apply for certain technical positions can be experienced as a barrier. Offline and online forms of mentoring can help women overcome these obstacles, get information about which skills really matter for the job and reach decision-making positions in journalism and tech.

Feminist hackathons

The word hackathon is a combination of the words 'hack' and 'marathon' (Boyles, 2017). These events are frequent in computer programmer and hacker communities and articulate several elements of the hacker ethic. First of all, hackathons provide spaces for innovation, being creative with technology and finding solutions for specific problems. In other words, there is a focus on experimentation, tinkering and exchanging technological skills. Second, collaboration is important, and participants usually work in teams with members of different backgrounds to deliver projects. Some hackathons are organised as a competition where the best ideas receive a prize. In Chapter 3, I have discussed how hackathons also provide structures for socialising and interaction between journalists and computer programmers, developers and designers, which can lead to exchanges in cultural values. At journalism hackathons, the aim is usually to generate innovative ideas on how to create, disseminate and consume media and develop new news products and prototypes.

Hackathons function as learning spaces where journalists can accumulate digital capital and people from the technology field can become more acquainted with journalistic routines which can be a starting point for collaborative projects. Despite the idea of openness, which is often one of the founding principles of these events, not all journalists seem to have equal access to these opportunities. Several interviewees indicated that hackathons are not necessarily inclusive spaces, but rather tend to be predominantly white, heterosexual and male. This lack of diversity is an obstacle, especially for female journalists, LGBTQ+ journalists and people of colour to participate, but there are also other factors that can limit diversity at those events.

In Chapter 2, I mentioned gendered issues related to the time when hackathons are organised. These events are often held on weekends or after working hours, which intersects with the gendered work-life balance issue and can be a reason why journalists with caring responsibilities do not participate. And there is a second time element that has to do with the duration of these events. Most hackathons last only 24, 36 or 48 hours and this time constraint can result in the image that it requires intense and constant coding and participants need to have a high level of skills to be able to finish projects in a short period (Decker, Eiselt, & Voll, 2015). Moreover, research by Richterich (2017) on project development practices and technology use at hackathons showed that competitive incentives and time pressure result in a tendency in which time for learning new skills is limited since teams want to be as efficient as possible. Efficiency in this context means that tasks are divided based on the use of the existing capabilities of team members. This had a gender dimension since technical tasks were often given to men who had previous programming skills and tasks for design and giving presentations were commonly given to women. The study concluded that to make hackathons more inclusive "organisers would need to provide incentives for personal skills development rather than foster an environment that privileges efficient skills utilisation" (p. 13).

In response to the issues mentioned above, several hackathons have been organised based on feminist principles and specifically aimed at creating safe spaces in which journalists can increase their digital skills and interact with a diverse group of judges and mentors. Two examples are Cracking the Code (IWMF) and the Women's hackathon at USC Annenberg.

In 2015, the International Women's Media Foundation organised the Women's Digital News Entrepreneurs Summit in New York titled 'Cracking the Code' aimed at women entrepreneurs working in the digital news space (IWMF, 2019). In addition to seminars and lectures on barriers for women in digital media, there was also a day-long hackathon at the summit. The event wanted to bring female technologists, entrepreneurs and news media professionals together to develop applications and find technical solutions for gender inequality and problems experienced by women entrepreneurs in digital media. The underlying feminist aim was to support women in the media industry and encourage them not only to be users but also producers of innovation. Just like Chicas Poderosas and WanaData, it created a community of practice that helps female journalists build and share digital knowledge. The best prototypes were awarded cash prizes and support for further development. The first place went to TrollBusters, an initiative for countering online harassment of journalists developed by Michelle Ferrier, Louisa Reynolds, Sneha Inguva, Debbie Galant and Berta Valle, which will be discussed further in Chapter 5. Other winning ideas for applications helped women digital media entrepreneurs to pitch ideas, visualised the gender of reporters and paired young women with successful female mentors.

A second series of hackathons to empower women in media and technology was organised by MediaShift in collaboration with different higher education institutions (MediaShift, 2019). In 2015, the USC Annenberg School for Communication and Journalism held a weekend-long event called 'Hack the Gender Gap' for female undergraduate and graduate students with a focus on immersive journalism (USC Annenberg, 2015). After an introductory lecture with women in top positions in media and tech, students worked in teams to create their start-up ideas around immersive journalism and virtual reality and presented them to judges on the last day. MediaShift organised similar hackathons in October 2014, April 2016 and November 2017 in collaboration with the Reed College of Media at West Virginia University with a focus respectively on wearables, hardware and artificial intelligence in media. Mark Glaser, who was one of the organisers, explained that the aim was to offer women a space to be creative and entrepreneurial and take power over every stage of the development process. The entire team of mentors, speakers and judges consisted of women and men only had supporting roles. To make it a safe space, each team had a mentor to offer advice or intervene in case of sexism, racism or other forms of intolerant behaviour.

Redefining nerd stereotypes

All initiatives described in the previous paragraphs provide areas where alternative narratives on gender and technology can be developed. Several female interviewees proudly identified as geeks or nerds and used these labels to describe themselves on social media platforms and website biographies. To some, this was an act of resistance aimed at giving new meanings to these words and creating alternative representations that challenge the stereotypical image of nerds as a white, anti-social, heterosexual and male. For example, a 32-year-old female founder of a news start-up saw a need for other representations of being a nerd in journalism and technology and proposed an alternative image based on what it means to be a nerd to her that goes against the belief that someone good in technology is by definition anti-social and sacrifices a big part of their life to programming:

> I am proudly nerdy. One of the reasons that I love journalism, in general, is because it always allows me to explore a ton of different interests. To do that in a lot of different ways. To me, it is a big draw to be in this industry because I can dive really deep into something that I am curious about or I can explore a lot of issues. That is part of my

> personality and when I say nerd, what I mean is that I am a naturally very curious person and that I get really caught up in that curiosity.

These ways in which female journalists are redefining what it means to be a nerd were empowering to other women in the study. Seeing other women who are working in 'the geeky part of journalism' inspired them to build a career in those areas. An example of this is a 31-year-old female data journalist who described the experience of meeting other female nerds at hackathons:

> At hackathons, you mostly see men. You see more and more women in data journalism and more women who are coding, and that's really nice. You see this woman with red hair, really beautiful who says: I am fluent in programming in this and that language, and she is just a complete nerd you know! I am always a bit surprised by that, but it's nice to have these alternative representations.

By self-labelling as a nerd, female journalists were reclaiming nerd stereotypes and encouraging other women to create their own alternative narratives on gender and technology. In this way, being a nerd in journalism can move beyond the association with being socially awkward and utterly devoted to technology toward an understanding of a nerd as someone who is deeply involved in using technology for social purposes and creating high-quality journalism.

Feminist views on challenging and reproducing gender inequality

In this chapter, we saw how female journalists use digital capital in a strategy aimed at empowerment. By participating in feminist hackathons and building networking and mentoring relationships, women are increasing their digital expertise and confidence, actively questioning the gender order in journalism and creating spaces for collective support, solidarity and action. These spaces provide a foundation for developing strategies to challenge the gendered doxa of journalism. Moreover, by using these strategies, women in the study were 'doing gender differently' by expressing their passion for technology and demonstrating their skills in a way that did not confirm the dominant gender ideology (Kelan, 2007). This goes against Bourdieu's deterministic belief that women accept their own subordination in their minds and confirm it in their actions. On the contrary, many interviewed women had a strong feminist consciousness, were aware of their subordinated position in journalism and actively wanted to change it.

It takes more than nuclear physics

It is interesting to look at these results in the light of discussions in feminist media studies on the reproduction and transformation of the gender status quo in journalism. The dominant assumption in the earliest research was that when women reached a representation of roughly one-third of all newsroom staff, they would form a 'critical mass' and be able to counterbalance the dominant male organisation culture, news practices and news content (Eisenstein, 1981; Gallagher, 1995; Mills, 1997). The idea of a critical mass goes back to nuclear physics, where it refers to the amount that is needed to start a chain reaction (Dahlerup, 2005). Critical mass theory, however, was heavily criticised for being too simplistic and based on essentialist beliefs about the reporting of male and female journalists (Steiner, 2012; van Zoonen, 1988). The proposed solution to 'add women and stir' left subtle mechanisms that sustain gender inequality in newsrooms intact. Even in countries where the critical mass threshold is exceeded, the expected chain reaction did not occur.

One of the reasons why the influx of women in journalism professions and education will not automatically lead to changes in newsroom culture and the status of women that is often given is that female journalists are gender blind, not aware of the relevance of gender mechanisms in their work environments, and reproduce gender inequality (Gillwald, 1994; Goward, 2006; Ross, 2001). This way of reasoning is similar to Bourdieu's conceptualisation of gender as "sexually characterised habitus" (p. 3) and his presentation of gender division as doxic that leaves limited room for change. The process of professional socialisation, during which journalists are familiarised with journalism's professional values and norms, is accorded an essential role in the unconscious adoption, internalisation and normalisation of the male-identified concerns of a male profession (Elmore, 2007; Ross, 2001). These views portray female journalists as rather passive since they are merely undergoing a process of socialisation with rather pessimist perspectives on the possibility of change in the future.

Other takes on how the gender order is reproduced in journalism that use Bourdieu's concepts position men and women in journalism in an opposing and hierarchical relationship in which men are the dominant and women the subordinated group (Melin, 2008; Tsui & Lee, 2012). Strategies of female journalists to navigate the field are expressed as a matter of aggregating either male or female capital. Female journalists who are working in news areas that are considered traditionally male, for example, hard news or sports journalism or showing attitudes and behaviour that would be stereotypically attributed to men such as being direct and aggressive are believed to follow the 'one of the boys strategy' which is aimed at countering the negative cultural capital of being female by aggregating male capital (Melin, 2008; Ross, 2001; van Zoonen, 1998a; Zuiderveld, 2011). Women who accept their subordinated roles in news beats that are associated with low status are assumed to follow the 'marionette strategy' or the 'woman journalist strategy' (Melin-Higgins, 2004; van Zoonen, 1998b). Both are considered strategies of assimilation with the male norm in journalism. The exception to this is the 'one of the girls strategy' which challenges the gender order because the female journalists who use it are believed to maximise their female capital and try to use it positively. For example, by increasing the status of so-called "women's themes" and creating space for alternative voices and feminist issues.

Beyond "boys" and "girls"

Descriptions such as being 'one of the boys' or 'one of the girls' feel out of tune with the complex experiences of journalists interviewed in this study. Female journalists are not trying to be 'one of the boys' by entering in technologically-driven areas of journalism but are actively redefining those areas to be more inclusive. Also, in line with this, digital capital cannot be equated with male capital. Ideas of separate forms of male and female capital go back to feminist theorists who added and theorised gender dispositions as a distinct form of capital based on Bourdieu's statement that cultural capital refers to embodied dispositions that were described in the introductory chapter (Huppatz, 2012; Lovell, 2000; McCall, 1992; Skeggs, 2004). Moi (1991) proposes a valuable alternative conceptualisation of gender as a form of symbolic capital that interacts with other types of capital and has a different value depending on the context. This allows for a more flexible and less deterministic view of the creation and recreation of the gender order and of women as active agents who compete for the same kinds of capital as men. Djerf-Pierre (2005) has built on Moi's (1999) appropriation of Bourdieu concerning media management and confirmed the assumption that women counteract their negative gender symbolic capital by amassing other kinds of capital. She found that female decision-makers had more educational capital and social capital than their male counterparts, which was confirmed in my study, while also adding digital capital to the equation.

Many female journalists had more difficulties in translating their digital capital in symbolic capital because it is evaluated based on perceptions and evaluations, which are patterned by cultural beliefs about gender. The legitimacy of their digital capital is often questioned. Linked with this, women feel less confident about their digital skills and are less vocal about their expertise, which implies that they cannot convert their digital capital into the same opportunities for recruitment and career advancement as men. By participating in networks and mentoring relationships, several female journalists were increasing their social capital, gaining self-confidence and trying to overcome these obstacles.

Although community building, networking and mentoring among female journalists are valuable for capital building and developing structures of solidarity and collaboration, these strategies should be applied to newsrooms to change the gendered structure of journalism. The last chapter of this book will talk about how news organisations can be an ally in the struggle for gender equality. Gender equality will also have to be story that is supported by female and male journalists. It is important to take into account that advancement toward more equality will not be a static process from one point to another. Policies that are developed for more gender-equal newsrooms will have to take into account potential setbacks. The next chapter will show how traditional gender obstacles that are appearing in modified forms in the digital spaces of journalism can slow the progress that has been made over the years.

References

Boyles, J. L. (2017). Laboratories for news? Experimenting with journalism hackathons. *Journalism*. doi:10.1177/1464884917737213

Chicas Poderosas. (2019). *About*. Retrieved from https://chicaspoderosas.org/about/

Dahlerup, D. (2005, September). *The theory of critical mass revised*. Paper presented at the annual meeting of the American Political Science Association, Washington, DC.

Decker, A., Eiselt, K., & Voll, K. (2015, October). *Understanding and improving the culture of hackathons: Think global act local*. Paper presented at the IEEE Frontiers in Education Conference, El Paso, TX.

Digital Women Leaders. (2019). *About*. Retrieved from www.digitalwomenleaders.com/about

Djerf-Pierre, M. (2005). Lonely at the top: Gendered media elites in Sweden. *Journalism*, *6*(3), 265–290.

Eisenstein, Z. (1981). *The radical future of liberal feminism*. New York, NY: Longman.

Elmore, C. (2007). Recollections in hindsight from women who left: The gendered newsroom culture. *Women and Language*, *3*(2), 18–27.

Gallagher, M. (1995). *An unfinished story: Gender patterns in media employment*. Paris, France: UNESCO.

Gillwald, A. (1994). Women, democracy and media in South Africa. *Media Development*, *2*(94), 27–32.

Goward, P. (2006). Gender and journalism. *Pacific Journalism Review*, *12*(1), 15–19.

Huppatz, K. (2012). *Gender capital at work: Intersections of femininity, masculinity, class and occupation*. London, UK: Palgrave Macmillan.

IWMF. (2019). *Home*. Retrieved from www.iwmf.org/

Kelan, E. K. (2007). Tools and toys: Communicating gendered positions towards technology. *Information, Communication & Society*, *10*(3), 358–383.

Lovell, T. (2000). Thinking feminism with and against Bourdieu. *Feminist Theory, 1*(1), 11–32.
McCall, L. (1992). Does gender fit? Bourdieu, feminism, and conceptions of social order. *Theory and Society, 21*(6), 837–867.
MediaShift (2019). *MediaShift events.* Retrieved from http://mediashift.org/mediashift-events/
Melin-Higgins, M. (2004). Coping with journalism: Gendered newsroom culture. In M. de Bruin & K. Ross (Eds.), *Gender and newsroom culture: Identities at work* (pp. 197–222). Cresskill, NJ: Hampton Press.
Melin, M. (2008). *Gendered journalism cultures: Strategies and tactics in the field of journalism in Britain and Sweden* (Unpublished doctoral dissertation), University of Göteborg, Göteborg, Sweden.
Mills, K. (1997). What difference do women journalists make? In P. Norris (Ed.), *Women, media, and politics* (pp. 41–50). Oxford, UK and New York, NY: Oxford University Press.
Moi, T. (1991). Appropriating Bourdieu: Feminist theory and Pierre Bourdieu's sociology of culture. *New Literary History, 22*(4), 1017–1049.
Moi, T. (1999). *What is a woman?* Oxford, UK: Oxford University Press.
Richterich, A. (2017). Hacking events: Project development practices and technology use at hackathons. *Convergence.* doi:10.1177/1354856517709405
Ross, K. (2001). Women at work: Journalism as en-gendered practice. *Journalism Studies, 2*(4), 531–544.
Skeggs, B. (2004). Introducing Pierre Bourdieu's analysis of class, gender and sexuality. In L. Adkins & B. Skeggs (Eds.), *Feminism after Bourdieu* (pp. 19–33). Oxford, UK: Blackwell.
Steiner, L. (2012). Failed theories: Explaining gender differences in journalism. *The Review of Communication, 12*(3), 201–223.
Tsui, C. Y. S., & Lee, F. L. F. (2012). Trajectories of women journalists' career in Hong Kong. *Journalism Studies, 13*(3), 370–385.
USC Annenberg. (2015, October). *Women's hackathon hack the gender gap.* Retrieved from https://annenberg.usc.edu/file/womens-hackathon-hack-gender-gap
van Zoonen, L. (1988). Rethinking women and the news. *European Journal of Communication, 3*(1), 35–53.
van Zoonen, L. (1998a). A professional, unreliable, heroic marionette: M/F: Structure, agency and subjectivity in contemporary journalism. *European Journal of Communication, 1*(1), 123–143.
van Zoonen, L. (1998b). One of the girls? The changing gender of journalism. In C. Carter, G. Branston, & S. Allan (Eds.), *News, gender and power* (pp. 33–46). London, UK and New York, NY: Routledge.
WanaData. (2019). *WanaData.* Retrieved from https://codefornigeria.org/wanadata/
Zuiderveld, M. (2011). Hitting the glass ceiling – Gender and media management in Sub-Saharan Africa. *Journal of African Media Studies, 3*(3), 401–415.

5 From bytes to backlash

Whenever journalists are hacking the gender gap and making significant progress in obtaining equal rights and opportunities, we have to be attentive to mechanisms aimed at reversing those achievements. The previous chapters have shown how technology is related to several possibilities to go beyond the gendered structures of traditional journalism, but at the same time, comes with new gendered challenges. This chapter will focus on how gendered obstacles are emerging in adjusted forms in digital spaces of journalism.

Digital spaces offer new publishing platforms for media organisations as well as tools for journalists to gather and disseminate information. They can be used for contacting sources, engaging with audiences, networking and doing research for stories (Chadha & Wells, 2016; Hedman & Djerf-Piere, 2013; Hermida, 2010). At the same time, these platforms have made journalists more vulnerable to digital threats that come in different shapes and forms such as digital surveillance, disinformation, cyber-attacks and online intimidation (Henrichsen, Betz, & Lisosky, 2015).

Studies have shown that online harassment is a gendered issue. Female journalists are disproportionally confronted with misogynist comments, verbal and physical threats, cyberstalking and sexual harassment online. A survey of the International Federation of Journalists (2018) pointed out that more than two-thirds of the female journalists who are harassed online are attacked based on their gender. A significant part of the harassment that women were already experiencing offline has moved to online spaces (Barton & Storm, 2013; Mijatović, 2016). A global study of 597 women journalists and media workers conducted by TrollBusters and the IWMF indicated that slightly more female participants were threatened or harassed online than reported physical threats or harassment (Ferrier, 2018).

Understanding the dynamics of online harassment is essential, in particular in the context of journalism, because it can have a chilling effect on free speech, reduce the freedom of the press, and create environments in which journalists self-censure (Edström, 2014). In both surveys mentioned above, approximately four out of ten women avoided reporting specific stories after being harassed online. Additionally, online harassment can have a considerable psychological and emotional impact and prevent journalists from doing their job and making use of the professional advantages of digital platforms.

Although online abuse tends to be positioned as a completely new phenomenon that occurred because of digitalisation and as a side effect that comes with the anonymity of the Internet, there are many parallels with offline harassment in journalism. Just like offline sexual harassment, online harassment is both a symptom and a cause of inequalities and patriarchal structures in the media industry. Sexual harassment can be seen as a manifestation of gendered hierarchies and the abuse of power that is related to them, and at the same time, it sustains unequal gendered power relationships by pushing women out of the industry and limiting their career development. In several ways, online harassment is the flip side of the same coin. It reflects and amplifies dynamics that operate in the offline world of journalism. Therefore, it should not be seen as a novel challenge but rather as a continuation of traditional forms of bias and discrimination in journalism.

This chapter is based on 23 qualitative interviews with journalism professionals between 24 and 72 years old who have experienced different forms of online harassment (18 women, 5 men). They are working in different media sectors and on various news beats, mostly as journalists or columnists. Most participants were employed (13) or freelancing (9), and one journalist combined both. The research offers insights into their experiences of online harassment and the strategies they use to deal with this. Considering that in digital spaces, not only misogynist but also racist, homophobic, transphobic, ageist and other harmful discourses can be openly expressed, the analysis will pay attention to how different forms of oppression can amplify each other online.

Digital spaces in journalism

The introduction of digital platforms changed the playing field in the news industry (Bell & Owen, 2017; Nielsen & Ganter, 2018). With the traditional business model under pressure, news companies became increasingly dependent on online activities for revenues and audience engagement (Wahl-Jorgensen et al., 2016). At the same time, new digital-native news outlets are competing with them for clicks and traffic. In this context, news organisations opened their online platforms to comments from the audience. The comment sections that were introduced in the beginning on news websites have recently moved more and more to social media platforms (Hermida & Thurman, 2008; Jönsson & Örnebring, 2011).

Digital spaces do not only provide new ways of collecting capital for news organisations but also for journalists. First of all, interviewed journalists use online platforms to increase their cultural capital by demonstrating their expertise and skills in certain areas. Getting recognised as an expert online can result in invitations to give lectures, moderate debates and participate in panels. A 35-year-old female freelancer who was one of the only English speaking writers in her country used her blog to connect with an international audience. This last point can be linked to social capital as well, which journalists can gather online by interacting with their audiences, colleagues and sources (Molyneux & Holton, 2015; Molyneux & Mourão, 2019). Additionally, digital platforms offer opportunities to increase economic capital (Hanusch & Bruns, 2017). For employed journalists, having a strong online presence functions as a safety net in an unstable, problematic and precariat media labour market characterised by budget cuts and lay-offs. For freelancers, it plays a vital role in advertising skills to future employers and attracting new clients and assignments. A 34-year-old female freelancer expressed it this way:

> It's like a megaphone where 13,000 people are listening. You don't just throw that away. It is a business capital for me. I am not just going to run away from that. Especially not when I also have to sell articles and books. It is much harder to tell someone who has 13,000 followers that you don't want their articles any more than to someone with 500 followers. I am very conscious of that.

All these forms of capital can be translated into symbolic capital. Research has indicated that social media play an essential role for journalists to establish status in their profession and build credibility and reputation online (Mourão, 2015). In this respect, several interviewees added that digital spaces especially give more visibility and status to the work of women in journalism and topics related to gender issues and feminism that usually do not receive a lot of space in traditional news media. For example, the MeToo hashtag provided an excellent tool for speaking the unspeakable about sexual misconduct.

#MeToo allowed women to break the silence and raise their voices on issues that are generally surrounded by an aura of taboo. Those voices are not only often ignored but also misrepresented in the mainstream media. Sexual violence is mostly represented as an individualised, 'women's issue' that belongs to the private sphere and is not high on the news agenda. In relation to sexual harassment and assault, media reporting is characterised by mechanisms of gender bias that blame victims, excuse perpetrators and promote stereotypes of women. In this sense, social media were an important ally to a movement that was aimed at bringing light to these issues by providing alternative spaces where these topics could be debated. Even more so, women could tell these stories in their own words and deliver alternative narratives about misogyny, power and inequalities. The aftermath of the hashtag did not stay limited to digits of zeros and ones in online spaces but even reached the highest levels of the media industry as high-placed men had to quit their positions.

These insights can be linked to optimist views on the liberating and empowering potential of digital spaces. Several authors believe that it can make journalism more democratic and the journalist-audience relationship a more reciprocal one (Loader & Mercea, 2011). On this reasoning, online spaces are even seen as a digital manifestation of Habermas' public sphere in which citizens engage in an open, rational dialogue, raise concerns and share different views on societal and political issues (Papacharissi, 2004). In relation to gender, this is often connected to the expectation of increased opportunities for women who are historically excluded from the public sphere to raise their voices in public debates and support feminist political action and protest (Drüeke & Zobl, 2016; Megarry, 2014).

Although social media platforms provide spaces where stories of sexual harassment can be shared, it is important to note that they do not offer safe spaces to do so. Gardiner (2018, p. 601) highlights that online interaction is "far from the idealised vision of a mutually beneficial conversation between journalists and their readers". Several studies have pointed out that this is prevented by 'offensive comments', 'antisocial behaviour' and 'toxic conversation', often put under the umbrella term 'incivility' in studies on news comments (Coe, Kenski, & Rains, 2014; Muddiman & Stroud, 2017). This label, however, is blind to misogynistic, racist, homophobic and other harmful elements that are frequently part of online discourse and the underlying power dynamics that sustain inequalities in journalism (Jane, 2014).

Experiences of online harassment

The interviews with journalists on their experiences of harmful discourse online shed light on the intensity, scope and intersectional aspects of this phenomenon. Online attacks happened through a wide range of channels ranging across online comment sections of news websites to individual exchanges via private e-mail or broad publication via social media. Perpetrators were perceived to be individuals, collectives, or even states and acted anonymously or in their own name.

Experiences of harassment differed reflecting gender, both in terms of content and severity. When asked about the kinds of harassment they are facing, male interviewees receive more comments on the content of articles, the validity of their arguments and political partiality, whereas female interviewees encountered more personal and sexualised comments with rape threats, references to their appearance and stereotypical ideas about the position of women in society. In the following quote, a 28-year-old female freelance journalist imagined what it would be like to be a male journalist to illustrate this gendered difference:

> If I would be a man, maybe I would get reactions from trolls when I publish something, but it would not be so personal. I never saw somebody online say to my male colleagues: 'you should be raped' or 'you are too ugly to be raped'. It seems like there is always a certain level of basic respect when they address a male journalist. They say, for example, 'you are crazy' or 'you forgot to take your pills today', but it is much less aimed at their gender.

The growing threat to the safety of female journalists has been put on the agenda by several organisations such as the Organization for Security and Co-operation in Europe, Amnesty International, the International Federation of Journalists and the International Association of Women in Radio and Television. However, gender is not the only aspect of identity that plays a role in experiences of online harassment and online misogyny is amplified by other harmful discourses such as ageism, racism and homophobia.

Ageism was only experienced by women in the study and went in two directions. Younger women, on the one hand, were told that they have no credibility and lack the expertise to have a valid opinion certain topics, whereas older female journalists received comments saying that they are too old and too ugly to have anything to contribute to the debate. Both aspects are illustrated in the following quotes of an older and younger female journalist:

> Age was a reoccurring factor actually. They told me that I am young, that I don't know what I am talking about, that I have no credibility to write on the issues that I was writing, that I don't even have a proper education.
>
> (35-year-old female freelancer)

> I constantly get told that I am too old to have an opinion on things. That I am always whining and that I should keep my mouth shut. It's like when you pass a certain age, you cannot have a valid opinion anymore.
>
> (72-year-old female journalist and columnist)

This raises two concerns about the future of gender in journalism. First, as discussed in Chapter 1, women are highly underrepresented in higher age groups, which is often linked to their early departure from the profession, particularly when they have children. Online harassment, however, has to be taken into account as another factor that can push women out of journalism. Especially on the screen, women are disappearing after a certain age because of stereotypes based on the assumption that they are not young and attractive enough anymore. Being in a visible position in journalism comes with an increased vulnerability to online abuse as well. Ageist and sexist comments on social media from the audience can be a legitimation for news companies to sustain these discriminatory practices.

Second, it is necessary to make a link with experiences of work conditions in journalism. Research has shown that both gender and age play a role in being at risk for burnout in journalism (Reinardy, 2009, 2011). Contrary to what might be expected, young journalists report high rates of exhaustion, are most 'at risk' of burnout, and express more intentions to leave the profession. When looking at gender, female journalists report higher levels of burnout, exhaustion and lower levels of professional efficacy than male journalists. Online harassment is an additional stress factor that can intensify the pressure on journalists in an already challenging and demanding work environment. Taking all these circumstances into account prompts the conclusion that women, especially women in young age groups, are a high-risk group for burnout and more disposed to leave the profession. A survey by Ferrier (2018) shows that younger journalists and media workers (18–39) (36%) were twice as likely to cite experiencing online harassment as a reason for thinking about quitting journalism than journalists older than 40 (18%). A 35-year-old female participant explained to me how being confronted with online harassment when she started out in journalism felt overwhelming because she did not know how to cope and felt alone in her struggle. Gradually she learned to distance herself from the harassment as she became more experienced both as a journalist and as someone who is targeted by online abuse.

For several interviewees, a considerable part of the abuse they are receiving online is homophobic. Both male and female journalists who are openly gay frequently received comments on their sexuality and appearance. Homophobia and misogyny were closely linked in those experiences. For example, a 34-year-old female freelancer and columnist who identified as queer claimed:

> Most people can see that I am not straight, and they have difficulties with my boyish looks and the fact that I identify as queer. They really dislike that. Then I get a lot of dirty dyke this, dirty man that.

The negative comments that were received because of having a sexuality that differs from the heterosexual norm are wrapped in critiques on an appearance that does not conform to normative ideals of female beauty. Similarly, gay male journalists received comments that they look or sound too feminine. This illustrates how homophobia and misogyny online work together to sustain patriarchy. This discourse tells us that femininity is considered inferior to masculinity and that crossing the boundaries of the very narrow definitions of what it means to be 'a real man' and 'a real woman' is not tolerated. Homophobic discourse was also used to discredit the opinion of journalists who identified as heterosexual. Female journalists writing about feminist issues were often called a lesbian online, whereas male journalists writing about masculinity were called gay, a sissy, faggot or a pussy. The use of 'gay' and 'lesbian' as pejorative terms sustains the idea that the opinion of LGBTQ+ journalists online is not valid.

Both male and female journalists were confronted with racism online. Journalists of colour were told that they should 'go back to their roots' and 'leave the country' even if they were born and raised in that country. For female journalists of colour, it felt like being under a double attack since racism amplified the misogyny they were already experiencing. Racist comments were expressed to journalists that had a foreign-sounding last name in their country of residence as well. A 28-year-old female online journalist who was attacked for this reason talked about differences in her experience of racism and sexism online. She explained that misogyny became a normalised aspect of her life because she grew up with it as a child, whereas online, she experienced racism for the first time. She felt like it was even more difficult to talk about racism because it is not taken seriously, and it is even a bigger taboo than sexism in society and in the newsroom.

These findings suggest that offline inequalities do not vanish in online spaces. Journalists who face discrimination because of different parts of their identities offline are targeted for the same identities on social media (Gardiner, 2018). In a sense, the dynamics and consequences of online harassment are quite similar to those of offline harassment, but whereas the emphasis of #MeToo was on making visible what happens behind closed doors, those kinds of discourses are widely available on the Internet. The next section compares the dynamics of online harassment with previous research on offline harassment to show that there are more similarities than differences between the two.

Normalisation

When asked about their reactions to online harassment, the majority of the interviewees explained that they try to ignore trolls or people harassing them online. Some of them used technical tools provided by social media platforms such as blocking or muting to help avoid such negative comments. This strategy went hand-in-hand with normalisation of online abuse. In this discourse, online harassment is seen as 'part of their job' or 'just another work routine' (Adams, 2018; Lewis, Rowe, & Wiper, 2017). Two elements contributed to this normalisation of online violence. The first involves the assumption that journalists should be able to deal with critique and that 'having a thick skin' is a job requirement. The second one is the belief that online violence is not the same as offline violence because it is virtual and does not have "real consequences" (Citron, 2014; Penny, 2013). Both aspects were expressed in the following comment by a 55-year-old male newspaper journalist:

> I never feel intimidated because I always make a difference between me as a person and my profession. I think that is also what people should do when they are confronted with these circumstances. You have to realise that the reason that you are being targeted has to do with the things that you do and not with the things that you are. . . . You can decide yourself to which degree you feel intimidated. It's part of our profession; if you cannot handle that, you have to do something else.

His strategy of ignoring online abuse came from a position of privilege. As a white, straight, male senior journalist, he received few remarks on aspects of his identity, which made it easier for him to differentiate between the professional and the personal. He generalises his own experience to all journalists, which makes him blind to systems of oppression related to online abuse. This became even more apparent later in the interview when he was asked what he would do if he received a personal attack:

> If they would do that I would really call for the police and file a complaint. For example, when someone says: 'We know where you live'. Even if it's just a joke, that's when I think you should give the signal that the boundary is there. But I have never experienced this.

For several female journalists, these types of personal comments were a daily reality. And even women who were frequently dealing with severe death and rape threats were in many cases seeing this as something they have to learn to live with in their job. These dynamics are similar to those informing experiences with offline sexual harassment (Claringbould, Knoppers, & Elling, 2004; de Bruin & Ross, 2004; Hardin & Shain, 2005; North, 2016; Steiner, 2009). Previous studies have shown that female journalists tend to accept sexual harassment as a normal part of the job and see it as the price they have to pay to work in a male-dominated environment.

The environment of the journalists played an important role either in reinforcing or questioning this strategy of normalisation. In some cases, the minimisation of the severity of online harassment was encouraged by colleagues in the newsroom, friends and family who were advising journalists 'not to care so much about it' and to 'get over it'. In other cases, the opposite was happening with people in their work and social environment trying to convince journalists that the online attacks they are experiencing are not normal and that they should file a complaint.

Minimisation and victim-blaming

Several female journalists who had tried to break this normalisation and questioned the ordinariness of online harassment by sharing their stories publicly had experienced forms of victim-blaming. Especially women writing on topics such as feminism, sexuality, migration or racism were told that they were 'asking for it' because they were covering 'controversial topics' that are 'a lightning rod for trolls'. A 28-year-old female freelancer recalled this reaction from people in her environment when she became targeted after writing about female sexuality online:

> They were saying: if you write something like that, you are looking for it. . . . A lot of people told me 'maybe you should be more careful'; 'imagine you are applying for a job and your future employer sees the reactions'; 'if I were you, I would watch out'. People often do not understand why I react to certain comments, and they tell me 'it's your own fault because you reacted' or tell me 'do not react to it', 'let it go' or 'ignore it'. I hate it when they do that. They might have good intentions, but for me, it's like, don't tell me how I should deal with people who harass me.

This made her doubt the legitimacy of her experiences and question the severity of the harassment. Victim-blaming is common in cases of offline harassment with references to the clothing or appearance of women being made as a justification for the harassment. The similarity in dynamics of victim-blaming in offline and online harassment is also highlighted by Penny (2013, p. 17), who refers to a woman's opinion online as "the short skirt of the Internet". #MeToo did not only put sexual harassment on the agenda but also showed the damaging impact that victim-blaming can have on the career of women who decided to come forward with their experiences, which can be a deterrent for people to share their stories in the future.

Underreporting

Both normalisation and victim-blaming are factors that contribute to the underreporting of online harassment. A survey of the IFJ (2018) showed that almost half of the women who suffered online harassment did not report it to management or the police. This is also found in research on offline harassment. Studies show that female journalists who experience sexual harassment do not report it because of fear of reprisal (Cho & Davenport, 2007), negative career consequences or the complaint is not handled in an adequate manner (North, 2016). Sexual intimidation is a taboo subject in newsrooms (De Clercq, 2002). It is present, but it remains invisible, which results in the conception that it is not a severe issue (Walsh-Childers, Chance, & Herzog, 1996). Compared to offline harassment, online harassment is more visible. However, most people remain passive bystanders and do not address perpetrators. A 35-year-old female freelancer indicated how this made it even more difficult for her to speak up about offline harassment:

> In the newsroom, you can scream and yell, and there could be a physical reaction, and you could at least feel a little bit better about yourself and try to respond to whatever you are being subjected to. . . . I think online, when you face this kind of harassment, whether it's verbal or sexual, there is no way to follow up with that.

Another obstacle is that the burden for gathering proof of online harassment often lies – just like with offline harassment – with the person who is under attack. Female journalists described how documenting online harassment involves a considerable amount of time and comes with a significant emotional toll. Even documenting and making screenshots of the harassments puts journalists in a constant negative spiral. In this context, Lewis et al. (2017) highlight the relevance of the concept of 'emotion work' introduced by Hochschild (1979) to refer to the labour involved in managing one's feelings to be appropriate for different situations. Their study of online abuse among women who debate feminist politics showed that women have to continually regulate their emotional reactions to minimise the negative impact of it, which is a psychologically intense and tiring process. Reporting abuse on social media diverts energy away from other tasks and typically does not result in long-term solutions. Interviewees mentioned that trolls were only temporarily blocked and were creative in making new profiles or no consequences were given to their requests for blocking.

Consequences

Even though online violence is often portrayed as not 'real life', it has concrete and very real consequences for those who are confronted with it. Online harassment has parallels with offline harassment in terms of consequences as well, in the sense that it decreases the opportunities of disadvantaged journalists and silences their voices (Megarry, 2014). Journalists who are harassed online are many times forced to delete their social media platforms, work under a pseudonym, or even leave journalism altogether.

Several journalists had considered quitting their jobs because of threats. However, this was not always a personal choice. In two cases, an editor decided to put female journalists on non-active to avoid putting the entire newsroom at risk. In an already-demanding profession, online harassment is an extra stress factor that can lead to psychological trauma, emotional harm and burnout. Several interviewees went into psychological therapy because of the impact of online harassment on their mental health and well-being. For most interviewed journalists, leaving social media was only 'the last option', which many of them did not consider because social media have become an indispensable part of their job. In some cases, their newsrooms were expecting them to be active on social media to spread stories and attract new audiences or to moderate the comments on social media platforms.

Furthermore, I talked earlier about how digital spaces offer opportunities for journalists to build capital. Online harassment can be linked to a negative impact on all those forms. The most obvious one is probably economic capital since it is evident that if journalists have to quit their job or are placed on non-active, they lose income. Moreover, freelancers who are dependent on social media for promoting their activities lose market value when going offline. Second, it diminishes the possibilities for gathering social capital because it has a negative impact on opportunities for networking and responding to comments of the audience (Adams, 2018). In this sense, online abuse disrupts the journalist-audience relationship. Finally, it also limits journalists from building cultural capital and demonstrating their expertise and can damage their reputation and credibility. This is illustrated in the following quote by a 28-year-old female freelance journalist who decided not to participate in television interviews about topics related to her expertise because of online harassment:

> When I am asked to talk about a piece on the radio or television, I ask myself: do I feel like the shitstorm that will follow? That is the first idea that goes through my mind. It is not so much 'will I be available' but

> more 'do I feel like that'? When I say yes to that, I am always wondering: won't I regret this?

This point should be taken into account in discussions on gender representation in media content. The Global Media Monitoring Project (2015), for example, shows that women are only 19% of the experts in the news media, which is confirmed in many other national and international studies. Many times this is explained based the premise that there are not enough female experts in specific fields or that they are challenging to find and hard to convince to be interviewed, which is not always the case. These results show that online violence also plays a role in the decisions of women not to share their expertise in the public debate and sustains the gendered representation of women and men in news topics. And there is also a link with the gendered division of labour in news production since several female interviewees decided not to report on news areas that tend to be male-dominated such as political, sports, music journalism or opinion writing because they were expecting a large number of harmful and abusive comments. All these dynamics contribute to the horizontal gender segregation in journalism.

Backlash

Online abuse does not only disrupt the professional and personal lives of journalists but also has consequences for civil society, democracy and the quality of journalism. Topics related to migration, feminism, racism and critical analysis of the politics and government of a country are triggers for all kinds of trolling, stalking, online hate speech, harassment and intolerant discourses (Butler, 1997; Jane, 2014). Journalists who work on these topics referenced the mental preparation they have to go through before publication. In some cases, they changed their writing because they felt the trolls reading over their shoulder or were engaging in self-censorship and decided not to cover those topics due to the abuse or the threat of it.

Abusive comments were aimed, not just at women, but at anyone defending gender equality. Female journalists adopting feminist positions who are trying to change the status quo (see Chapter 4) are particular targets. Stories on gender issues and feminism were not being covered because they were a red flag for online harassment. Cole (2015) draws on Foucault's concept of disciplinary rhetoric to indicate how violent anti-feminist discourse on social media serves to silence women who come forward as feminists in the public debate. This goes against the utopian beliefs in the liberating and empowering potential of a new, democratic digital sphere (Haraway, 1991; Plant, 1998), and suggests that that the online world replicates the gender inequalities of the offline world (Todd, 2017). This leads Jane, who defines online hostilities and sexualised threats as 'e-bile', to conclude that:

> While e-bile's medium is new, we can see that the e-bile message sits squarely within a far older tradition – one which insists that women are inferior; that their primary value relates to sexual utility; that they do not belong in the public sphere; and that those females who overstep the mark should be put 'back in their place' or otherwise punished.
>
> (Jane, 2016, p. 4)

In doing so, online harassment resembles the dynamics of a backlash. This concept was introduced in 1991 by Susan Faludi to describe the counter-assault that occurs when women have made significant progress in obtaining equal rights in society. Women have increased their presence in digital spaces, but online harassment constantly reminds them that they do not belong there (Jane, 2014). As female journalists challenge patriarchy offline and online, use social media to express feminist ideas and increase their digital capital for empowerment, there are mechanisms limiting the progress that is made (Lewis et al., 2017).

Resistance

Several women in the study had decided to speak out about their experiences of online harassment as a strategy of resistance. By openly communicating about their experiences, they were hoping to help other people who are experiencing online harassment to feel less alone. Interviewees inaugurated blogs to raise awareness about feminist topics and witnessed strong positive feedback from the public as an encouragement that keeps them going. For example, a 34-year-old female journalist and activist saw her blog as a learning opportunity in the struggle to fight offline gender harassment. For her, offline and online harassment were two sides of the same coin, so by observing how people expressed sexism online, she could learn about sexist thought patterns offline:

> If I remove or block people, then I don't see the problem. And I need to know what the problem is. Because whether we like it or not, the online world is a reflection of the offline world. And that research is what can help me in the future projects that I am trying to do. I use that as evidence.

An initiative that has been developed by journalists to tackle online harassment is TrollBusters (TrollBusters, 2019). This is a project that has been created at the Cracking the Code hackathon mentioned in Chapter 4. TrollBusters allows people who spot online violence or trolling to send a request to their website, which will result in support with personal endorsements, coaching and reputation repair services. This initiative also provides digital security training for journalists.

Conclusion

Strategies for dealing with online harassment mostly emerged bottom-up from individual journalists. While social media companies such as Facebook and Twitter emphasise the potential of their platforms for awareness-raising and empowerment, the tools they have developed to combat online harassment miss their goal, which creates an open field for online harassers. Journalists did not feel protected by those platforms. Most journalists were using blocking and muting options on social media, but they were insufficient because trolls were inventive in finding other ways to attack them. Also, most media companies have not developed solutions to this problem. When newsrooms decided to delete the comment section on their websites, the abuse shifted to their social media pages, and the roots were not addressed (Hermida & Thurman, 2008). Both for social media companies and for news companies, there are issues related to economic capital that prevent their ambitions to make this into safe space since even negative comments can have a positive impact on audience metrics. Newsrooms should move from passive bystanders to allies in the struggle to protect their journalists online.

References

Adams, C. (2018). They go for gender first: The nature and effect of sexist abuse of female technology journalists. *Journalism Practice*, *12*(7), 850–869.

Barton, A., & Storm, H. (2013). *Violence and harassment against women in the news media: A global picture*. International Women's Media Foundation & International News Safety Institute. Retrieved from www.iwmf.org/wp-content/uploads/2018/06/Violence-and-Harassment-against-Women-in-the-News-Media.pdf.

Bell, E., & Owen, T. (2017). *The platform press: How Silicon Valley reengineered journalism*. Retrieved from https://academiccommons.columbia.edu/catalog/ac:15dv41ns27.

Butler, J. (1997). *Excitable speech: A politics of the performative*. New York, NY and London, UK: Routledge.

Chadha, K., & Wells, R. (2016). Journalistic responses to technological innovation in newsrooms. *Digital Journalism*, *4*(8), 1020–1035.

Cho, S., & Davenport, L. D. (2007). Gender discrimination in Korean newsrooms. *Asian Journal of Communication*, *17*(3), 286–300.

Citron, D. K. (2014). *Hate crimes in cyberspace*. Cambridge, MA and London, UK: Harvard University Press.

Claringbould, I., Knoppers, A., & Elling, A. (2004). Exclusionary practices in sport journalism. *Sex Roles*, *51*(11–12), 709–718.

Coe, K., Kenski, K., & Rains, S. A. (2014). Online and uncivil? Patterns and determinants of incivility in newspaper website comments. *Journal of Communication*, *64*(4), 658–679.

Cole, K. K. (2015). It's like she's eager to be verbally abused: Twitter, trolls, and (en)gendering disciplinary rhetoric. *Feminist Media Studies*, *15*(2), 356–358.

de Bruin, M., & Ross, K. (2004). *Gender and newsroom cultures: Identities at work*. Cresskill, NJ: Hampton Press.

De Clercq, M. (2002, July). *Shedding light on absence: Women's underrepresentation in the newsroom*. Paper presented at the conference and general assembly of the International Association for Media Communication Research, Barcelona, Spain.

Drüeke, R., & Zobl, E. (2016). Online feminist protest against sexism: The German-language hashtag #aufschrei. *Feminist Media Studies*, *16*(1), 35–54.

Edström, M. (2014). Nordic journalism with gender parity and problems. In M. Edström & R. Molster (Eds.), *Making change: Nordic examples of working towards gender inequality in the media* (pp. 47–52). Göteborg, Sweden: Nordicom.

Faludi, S. (1991). *Backlash: The undeclared war against women*. London, UK: Vintage.

Ferrier. (2018). *Attacks and harassment: The impact on female journalists and their reporting*. Retrieved from www.iwmf.org/wp-content/uploads/2018/09/Attacks-and-Harassment.pdf

Gardiner, B. (2018). It's a terrible way to go to work: What 70 million readers' comments on the Guardian revealed about hostility to women and minorities online. *Feminist Media Studies*, *18*(4), 592–608.

GMMP. (2015). *Who makes the news? Global Media Monitoring Project*. London, UK: World Association for Christian Communication.

Hanusch, F., & Bruns, A. (2017). Journalistic branding on Twitter. *Digital Journalism*, *5*(1), 26–43.

Haraway, D. (1991). *Simians, cyborgs and women: The reinvention of nature*. New York, NY: Routledge.

Hardin, M., & Shain, S. (2005). Strength in numbers? The experiences and attitudes of women in sports media careers. *Journalism and Mass Communication Quarterly*, *82*(4), 804–819.

Hedman, U., & Djerf-Piere, M. (2013). The social journalist: Embracing the social media life or creating a new digital divide. *Digital Journalism*, *1*(3), 368–385.

Henrichsen, J. R., Betz, M., & Lisosky, J. M. (2015). *Building digital safety for journalists: A Survey of selected issues*. Paris, France: UNESCO.

Hermida, A. (2010). Twittering the news: The emergence of the ambient journalism. *Journalism Practice*, *4*(3), 297–308.

Hermida, A., & Thurman, N. (2008). A clash of cultures: The integration of user-generated content within professional journalistic frameworks at British newspaper websites. *Journalism Practice*, *2*(3), 343–356.

Hochschild, A. R. (1979). Emotion work, feeling rules, and social structure. *American Journal of Sociology*, *85*(3), 551–575.

International Federation of Journalists. (2018, November). *IFJ global survey shows massive impact of online abuse on women journalists*. Retrieved from www.ifj.org/media-centre/news/detail/article/ifj-global-survey-shows-massive-impact-of-online-abuse-on-women-journalists.html

Jane, E. A. (2014). Back to the kitchen, cunt: Speaking the unspeakable about online misogyny. *Continuum*, *28*(4), 558–570.

Jane, E. A. (2016). Online misogyny and feminist digilantism. *Continuum*, *30*(3), 284–297.

Jönsson, A. M., & Örnebring, H. (2011). User-generated content and the news: Empowerment of citizens or interactive illusion? *Journalism Practice*, *5*(2), 127–144.

Lewis, R., Rowe, M., & Wiper, C. (2017). Online abuse of feminists as an emerging form of violence against women and girls. *The British Journal of Criminology*, *57*(6), 1462–1481.

Loader, B. D., & Mercea, D. (2011). Networking democracy? Social media innovations and participatory politics. *Information, Communication & Society*, *14*(6), 757–769.

Megarry, J. (2014). Online incivility or sexual harassment? Conceptualising women's experiences in the digital age. *Women's Studies International Forum*, *47*(Part A), 46–55.

Mijatović, D. (2016). *New challenges to freedom of expression: Countering online abuse of female journalists*. Austria, Vienna: OSCE.

Molyneux, L., & Holton, A. (2015). Branding (health) journalism. *Digital Journalism, 3*(2), 225–242.

Molyneux, L., & Mourão, R. R. (2019). Political journalists' normalization of Twitter. *Journalism Studies, 20*(2), 248–266.

Mourão, R. R. (2015). The boys on the timeline: Political journalists' use of Twitter for building interpretive communities. *Journalism*, *16*(8), 1107–1123.

Muddiman, A., & Stroud, N. J. (2017). News values, cognitive biases, and partisan incivility in comment sections. *Journal of Communication*, *67*(4), 586–609.

Nielsen, R., & Ganter, S. A. (2018). Dealing with digital intermediaries: A case study of the relations between publishers and platforms. *New Media & Society*, *20*(4), 1600–1617.

North, L. (2016). Damaging and daunting: Female journalists' experiences of sexual harassment in the newsroom. *Feminist Media Studies*, *16*(6), 495–510.

Papacharissi, Z. (2004). Democracy online: Civility, politeness, and the democratic potential of online political discussion groups. *New Media & Society*, *6*(2), 259–283.

Penny, L. (2013). *Cybersexism: Sex, gender and power on the internet*. London, UK: Bloomsbury.

Plant, S. (1998). *Zeros and ones: Digital women + the new technoculture*. London, UK: Fourth Estate.

Reinardy, S. (2009). Female journalists more likely to leave newspapers. *Newspaper Research Journal, 30*(3), 42–57.

Reinardy, S. (2011). Newspaper journalism in crisis: Burn-out on the rise, eroding young journalists' career commitment. *Journalism, 12*(1), 33–50.

Steiner, L. (2009). Gender in the newsroom. In K. Wahl-Jorgensen & T. Hanitzsch (Eds.), *The handbook of journalism studies* (pp. 116–129). New York, NY: Routledge.

Todd, M. (2017). Virtual violence: Cyberspace, misogyny and online abuse. In T. Owen, W. Noble & F. C. Speed (Eds.), *New perspectives on cybercrime: Palgrave studies in cybercrime and cybersecurity* (pp. 141–158). London, UK: Palgrave Macmillan.

TrollBusters. (2019). *About us*. Retrieved from https://yoursosteam.wordpress.com/about/

Wahl-Jorgensen, K., Williams, A., Sambrook, R., Harris, J., Garcia-Blanco, I., Dencik, L., Cushion, S., Carter, C., & Allan, S. (2016). The future of journalism. *Digital Journalism, 4*(7), 809–815.

Walsh-Childers, K., Chance, J., & Herzog, K. (1996). Sexual harassment of women journalists. *Journalism & Mass Communication Quarterly, 73*(3), 559–581.

6 Conclusion

In this concluding chapter, I formulate an answer to the central question of the book: are traditional gender inequalities replicated in the new digital spheres of journalism or do they provide spaces that go beyond gender and other forms of bias? An additional question that follows from the feminist aim of my research is: how do we move forward from here? To answer these questions, the research findings will be integrated into a framework to move from change to disruption of inequalities in journalism with recommendations on how to hack the gender gap.

Replicating gender inequalities

In the introduction, I hinted that the answer to the main question would be more complicated than a simple and binary yes or no: technology presents both gendered challenges as well as opportunities for empowerment for women. It would be incorrect to conclude that there is a gendered digital divide in journalism that is comparable to the deeply rooted horizontal and vertical segregation, but the distinction that was made between 'hard' and 'soft' technical skills sounded familiar from a feminist perspective.

Programming, coding and development are commonly labelled as 'hard skills', whereas managing social media, negotiating with the marketing section, engaging with the audience and ensuring smooth communication in the team are labelled as soft skills. This difference is associated with a status differential. When asked which competencies are most important in an increasingly digitalised journalism environment, hard skills were positioned in first place and associated with greater status than soft skills. This dynamic also plays a role in the definition of technical positions. Coding, programming and development are immediately cited as examples of technical jobs and associated with high status, hiring and career opportunities, whereas audience development, product management and social media management, which also require a significant amount of technical competence, are not necessarily labelled explicitly as such and associated with lesser status in the newsroom.

We know from previous studies that status differentials in journalism tend to have a gender dimension, and this does not appear to be any different for digital skills and technology. Digital skills are evaluated based on gendered assumptions. In these evaluations, male journalists are expected to have more technical and rational skills, whereas female journalists are praised for softer skills such as bringing an emotional or human perspective to the story, being empathic and excellent in communication. This can lead to a gender division of tasks in journalism and technology with female journalists being pushed toward the 'softer' part and men picking up the 'hard' part in teams. Interviewees mentioned that coding, development and programming positions that are associated with high status tend to be male-dominated, whereas women are working more in social media management, product management and audience development that are associated with less status.

Future quantitative research on the representation of men and women in news production will need to update its definitions of positions to be able to offer insights into these new forms of gender segregation. In previous studies, technical jobs are approached as a single category and usually limited to positions that include camerawork, sound editing and lighting (Byerly, 2011; EIGE, 2013). My study shows that even within this category there are forms of gendered divisions among positions and that many new technical job titles could and should be added to the list to understand to full spectrum of gender in technology positions in journalism.

To explain the mechanisms that regulate gender divisions among these positions, it is necessary to go back to Chapter 1 and Acker's insights (1990, 1992) into how gendered expectations about jobs and skills sustain gendered structures in work organisations. We already knew that thinking in gendered dichotomies about the skills, preferences and abilities contributes to a gendered division of news beats, media sectors and positions in journalism. My research shows that when it comes to technology, gender is often thought of in zeros and ones as well. Because digital expertise is evaluated based on gender stereotypes, the skills of female journalists are considered as less legitimate and often doubted in the newsroom. This gender bias limits the opportunities for women to build careers in journalism and tech.

These gendered expectations are also expressed in images of what the ideal tech-savvy journalist looks like. Terms such as data ninjas, cowboys, superheroes, rockstars, wizards or nerds are increasingly part of the discourse on journalism and innovation, and even if they might sound exciting and challenging, not everyone can identify with them. Apart from the fact that many of those contain gendered language that evokes an image associated with masculinity, they also limit inclusiveness in other ways. The emphasis on differences instead of commonalities with traditional journalism and on having the right amount of technical skills makes it look like journalists need exceptional qualities to be able to work in journalism and technology. Besides, these are often defined as areas for 'nerds' and 'geeks' – an image that is associated with an assumption that journalists must make sacrifices in their social life to excel in technology.

Those high expectations have to be placed in a context in which journalists are experiencing an increased workload, expansion of their tasks and high demand for flexibility. Even though investing in digital skills can offer opportunities for recruitment and career advancement in a difficult media labour market, those skills mostly have to be gathered on weekends or after work hours which creates an advantage for journalists who can sacrifice leisure time to do so while disadvantaging those who cannot. The need to stay up-to-date with rapidly changing innovations increases the pressure on the work-life balance of journalists, especially for those who are already struggling to juggle the two and those with caring responsibilities. The traditional gendered work-life balance issue seems to play a role even in new fields of journalism and technology, and a division of household and care tasks based on traditional gendered role patterns can be a reason why female journalists have more difficulties and less time for developing and updating their digital skills.

Amplification of gender inequalities

Throughout the book, there are illustrations of interactions between journalism and technology in terms of the people working in them, work practices and cultural values. One of the questions raised about these exchanges is whether this means that forms of gender bias that are typical for the tech field will be reproduced in journalism.

The most obvious gendered consequence of these transitions comes down to the numbers. When more tech people are hired in journalism, this will probably not be beneficial for gender balance in the journalistic labour market simply because women are highly underrepresented in technological professions and education. Additional quantitative research can be helpful to gain insight into the educational and professional backgrounds of people working in journalism from a gender perspective. The findings of these studies will be relevant to include when numerical measurements of change and conclusions about gender developments based on statistics are made.

During my interviews, the lack of women in tech posts in journalism was often positioned as a direct consequence of the low number of women working in the tech field. However, placing this problem outside of journalism serves the idea that nothing can or should be done in journalism to improve gender issues. My study indicates that this is not the case. Apart from this quantitative aspect, there are subtle gendered obstacles in job descriptions, evaluations of skills, task divisions and learning spaces that should be addressed to make journalism and technology more inclusive. The next section focuses on how we can hack those barriers that are maintaining gender inequality in journalism.

Doing so is essential because gender inequalities in technology and journalism can amplify each other not only in employment but also in the news stories that are produced. Both news articles and code are written by humans. Even though code and data regularly have an aura of neutrality and objectivity, there are many choices involved in the way they are created, analysed and visualised. Just like the journalistic side of news is the result of a selection process about who will achieve a voice in the story, how the story will be framed and what will be the story focus, the tech side of news is the result of choices about how code is written, which databases are analysed and how the results will be presented. From previous studies, we know that the journalistic side commonly favours male perspectives, sources and topics (Byerly & Ross, 2006; GMMP, 2015). This is also the case for databases, which tend to contain more information on the lives and experiences of men than women (Criado-Perez, 2019). When data are increasingly used as a source for journalism without a critical reflection on this gender bias, it is possible that the invisibility of women in the news is amplified and we will get a very limited and biased sense of social reality. The same applies when social media are increasingly used to source news stories without taking into account that women's voices as well as critical and feminist perspectives are less represented in online spaces because of online harassment and digital threats.

Hacking the gender gap

The first step of hacking is identifying gaps in a system. This book offers insight into the many ways that gender inequality is limiting innovation and the quality of journalism. However, hacking is not only aimed at detecting bugs but also at finding ways to solve them. In Chapter 4, I talked about initiatives in which women are launching innovative projects for redesigning journalism based on feminist principles of solidarity, equality and collaboration. These have a great deal of potential to crack the coding ceiling in journalism. However, the responsibility for hacking the gender gap should not only be on those who are suffering disadvantages resulting from unequal structures. It will be necessary for both male and female journalists to recognise privileges they might be experiencing related to gender and other parts of their identities, understand disadvantages experienced by others and let this awareness guide their actions. The next section offers several recommendations for making technological advancement in journalism a more gender-equal story. There is a focus on questions such as how do we move forward from here, how can gender equality be a collaborative effort, and how can newsrooms become allies in the feminist struggle?

My research shows how ways of thinking from hacker, programmer and open-source communities are increasingly influencing journalism culture. This can propose new ways of doing journalism that are more in line with the increasingly digitalised media environment (Usher, 2016). The efficiency and timeliness of deeply rooted journalistic practices based on a lack of transparency on work methods, limited use of the possibilities of technology and data, and individualisation of the creative process are questioned by scholars and journalism practitioners. To some, rethinking journalism based on values of the open-source movement to include more participation, openness, iteration and collaboration will be essential to ensure its relevance in a context in which several pressures are challenging its authority, credibility and autonomy (Peters & Broersma, 2013).

In order to keep its authority and significance, journalism will not only need to keep up to date with technological advances and be more transparent and participatory but will also have to represent the diversity of societies. News that includes only the voices of a white, male, straight, cis-gendered, able-bodied elite is completely superseded. Decreases in audience reach and advertising revenues are commonly linked to the competition of news on social media and digital disruption, but what is often forgotten is that news is not appealing to a large part of the audience because it proposes a very stereotypical account of their lives. Diversity will be essential for news companies to survive in the current media landscape.

I would argue that values from hacker, programmer and open-source communities not only offer ways of rethinking journalism's main principles but can also be used to make journalism more inclusive and address structural inequalities in newsrooms. However, we know from Chapter 3 that hacker principles and values have a tendency to support the male status quo. That is why, before those values can be used as a foundation for a framework for disrupting gender inequalities in journalism, it is necessary to rethink them from a feminist perspective. In the next sections, I will explain how values of transparency, inclusiveness, experimentation, empowerment and iteration will be essential for a gender-equal future journalism.

Transparency

Openness is one of the central principles of hacker culture. It is grounded in the belief that information should be free and openly accessible to all to encourage the collective building and improvement of knowledge and innovations (Himanen, 2001). Transparency and full disclosure are essential in this process. This implies that code is publicly shared and open for anyone to use, change or expand. Articulations of this way of thinking are also found in new technologically-driven forms of journalism. For example, data journalists are sharing their methods and resources used to make a story with the public and with colleagues, even from competing newsrooms. Blogs, forums, tutorials and mailing lists open up the process behind the creation of news stories and provide help to solve technical problems. This approach is different from traditional journalism, where essential choices are usually made by an individual journalist and remain a black box to outsiders (Usher, 2016).

Transparency is not only crucial for hackers but also for hacking the gender gap. Many of the barriers sustaining gender and other inequalities in journalism can be linked somehow to a lack of transparency. For example, networking that happens in invisible and informal structures tends to favour a homogenous white, male group and can lead to the reproduction of inequality because outsiders do not have access to the knowledge of jobs and career advancement that is shared. Also, obscure recruitment and career advancement procedures create a window for all kinds of implicit bias and subjective criteria to sneak into the decision-making process and result in gender segregation. Finally, differences in payment based on gender or other characteristics remain under the radar if salaries are not publicly disclosed, making it difficult to negotiate a fair and equal payment and fight against the gender pay gap. For example, it was only after the government asked the BBC to disclose the salaries of on-air presenters with high earnings that Carrie Gracie, who was the China editor, found out that she was earning much less than male colleagues in similar positions and could start her campaign to denounce the pay discrimination.

In my study, transparency and openness were positively associated with diversity and gender equality in journalism and technology. Since many technologically-driven forms of journalism are still in development, there was a belief that they are still open to everybody, regardless of gender, age, ethnicity or other characteristics. The networks and communities that are being built around them were experienced as egalitarian and inclusive because knowledge is openly shared and accessible to anybody, which lowered the barriers to enter and participate, especially for female journalists and younger journalists.

Another aspect of this transparency is the importance of data for tracking and monitoring gender issues. This point was put forward in an open letter on how to end misogyny in the news industry written by ten international media leaders (Storm et al., 2018). Newsrooms that are open about what is being done to advance diversity and measure the progress that is made are essential in moving forward. There are examples of newsrooms in Sweden and the *Financial Times* in the United Kingdom that use automatic textual analysis to track the representativeness of news stories and diversity among sources that are included and give journalists real-time feedback on which voices have been covered, warning them when too many men are quoted. Opening data on diversity in newsrooms to the public can stimulate accountability and increase the credibility of journalism. We know from Chapter 1 that data can be a great tool to raise awareness on gender issues because it can spark public debate and creates opportunities to monitor issues over time. Sharing good practices and exchanging knowledge among different news organisations can help to build stronger and more efficient policies for equality.

I believe this is not only the case for newsrooms, but also for academic research on gender and media. In the first chapter, I explained how feminist research always has been closely related to feminist activism. I think that open access to data on gender and media and transparency about research methodologies can make those ties even stronger. It can be a starting point for new insights and inspire feminist action. A great deal of research material on gender issues is already out there but is not reaching a broad audience because it is only reported in specialised publications. This limits the possibilities for the collective building of knowledge and taking initiatives to address gender obstacles that come forward in research. I think there is much potential in collaborations between feminist academics and data journalists for placing gender issues such as gender-based violence, femicide and the gender pay gap on the agenda. The knowledge that has been gathered over the years by feminist scholars on methodologies and ways to study gender issues can be an added value in data journalism projects, while techniques from data journalism can be an essential add-on to traditional science communication to spread, translate and visualise results and to encourage awareness on gender issues and feminist topics.

Inclusiveness

This idea of openness in hacker culture goes hand in hand with the meritocratic belief that hackers are judged by their actions and skills rather than personal criteria such as degrees, age, race, gender, age, or position. In my study, a discourse of meritocracy was voiced in discussions of what is necessary to enter and build a career in new technologically-driven areas of journalism. Having the right digital skills was seen as the most decisive element in these processes. This was coupled with the assumption that since there is a very limited pool of people who have those skills in journalism, news companies cannot afford to pick and choose and discriminate between candidates based on characteristics such as gender, age or race. This was expected to lead to increased possibilities for female and minority journalists in these fields. Several female journalists entered data journalism because skills matter more than gender when topics are divided, and they had more access to hard news beats and investigative journalism. However, other results put this openness into a different perspective and indicate that new digital spaces and forms of journalism are not islands free of gender and other types of biases.

Openness is not the same as inclusiveness. Previous research has shown how discourses of meritocracy in many domains result in primarily white male-dominated communities, also in hacker groups, technology companies and newsrooms (Aldridge, 2001; Brooke, 2018; Löfgren-Nilsson, 2010; SSL Nagbot, 2016). Feminists emphasise that meritocracy is a myth if it is not backed up with an awareness of the relation of power, privilege and disadvantage that results in unequal opportunities. The idea that everybody is judged based on their skills and performance may look like an equal and fair arrangement, but in practice, it can sustain different forms of inequality and limit possibilities for change. In journalism, for example, a belief in objectivity, neutrality and impartiality can maintain stereotypes in the news because it is associated with the idea that journalists are merely documenting or reflecting the reality and nothing should be done to erase bias from reporting. The existence of sexism, racism, ageism and other often hidden biases work against this ideal of meritocracy. Different kinds of stereotypes sneak into evaluations and perceptions in work organisations, and this is no different in journalism and tech. A feminist perspective is necessary to recognise institutional and individual level privileges and challenge different layers of oppression (Shaw, 2014).

This viewpoint offers insight into several exclusionary mechanisms that are keeping talented people out of tech and journalism and limiting its diversity and inclusiveness. In this book, I mainly focused on gender diversity, but I also tried to offer insights into how privileges and disadvantages related to gender intersect with those related to other parts of identity such as age, sexuality or ethnicity. These intersectional aspects could be explored more in future research. For example, in studies on whether there are interactions between gender stereotypes and age stereotypes when it comes to assumptions on staying up-to-date with technology, on queer journalists' experiences at hackathons and on obstacles for women of colour in news start-ups and entrepreneurial journalism.

Experiences of interviewees who combine multiple disadvantages in journalism put the meritocratic principles into perspective. The skills-first approach in technologically-driven forms of journalism is sometimes translated in job advertisements with endless lists of programming languages, tools and applications in which applicants should excel. These high expectations are a barrier against entering the field, especially for female journalists and journalists from minority groups who often already felt like they do not belong in journalism and technology because of its lack of diversity. The next section discusses how this bias is attained but can be deleted from hiring and selection processes.

Experimentation

Hacking is not only about technical mastery but also about a spirit for tinkering, experimentation, continuous learning and problem-solving. In this sense, it is more about a mind-set than about a predefined set of skills. The focus in job advertisements on knowing a list of specific coding languages in combination with journalistic skills can keep people out who have the right mind-set but do not tick all the boxes. There is a gender dimension to this since previous research shows that women, in general, are less likely to apply for a job when they do not meet all the qualifications, whereas men apply more often even when they do not meet all the listed criteria. My study showed that female journalists tend to have a lower self-confidence about their technical competence and are more likely to underestimate their capabilities than male colleagues. Although gender inequality is frequently proposed as a supply problem related to the limited amount of people with tech skills that want to work in journalism, this also means that the full pool of talent is not being addressed.

Apart from avoiding gendered language in job applications that can unconsciously discourage female candidates from applying, the study offered insights into two other ways in which job descriptions can attract a more diverse group of applicants. First of all, job advertisements can explicitly mention that even candidates who do not meet all the qualifications are encouraged to apply. Several interviewees who are involved in the recruitment process had followed this strategy and booked positive results in their newsrooms. Second, keeping in mind that hacking and technological expertise are about continuous learning and not about a fixed set of skills and that technology is changing every day and skills are constantly having to be updated, job applications can refer to learning opportunities on the job to show candidates that they will be supported in building their talents.

Furthermore, instead of focusing too much on the advanced technical skills that employees have to bring into the job, newsrooms could benefit from providing internal structures for tinkering and experimenting with technology. A survey of the International Center for Journalists (2017) on the state of technology in global newsrooms showed that the demands of journalists for training in data journalism, cybersecurity, and web coding, design and development are higher than the opportunities available in newsrooms. My study shows that not all journalists have equal access to external training to stay up to date with all the latest technological advancement. Especially for female journalists, work-life balance, the lack of diversity at hackathons and the culture of these spaces were experienced as barriers.

In-house training for digital skills can take away some of the privileges and disadvantages related to the investment of time and resources in training outside of the newsroom. By having training sessions during working hours, newsrooms can create spaces in which men and women can experiment with new technologies and opportunities for more collaborative journalism practice. In Chapter 4, I discussed several examples of initiatives in which female journalists are building digital skills outside of the newsroom such as feminist-inspired hackathons, mentoring and networking efforts. These networks are valuable for women to expand the digital and social capital, share oppressive experiences, and find constructive solutions to deal with challenges both in a collective and individual way. The principles used to build these 'safe spaces' can be an inspiration to create a supportive newsroom environment that encourages openness and respect in which journalists can share their knowledge and learn from others – this means spaces that are inclusive, recognise power dynamics and privileges, and are based on structures of solidarity and not of competition, where sexism and other forms of discrimination are not tolerated, and where women have leading roles.

Empowerment

For hackers, technology is a means to an end, the end being achieving social change, safeguarding democracy, challenging injustices and empowering citizens. Similar ambitions were expressed by data journalists in my study. They used data in reporting as a vehicle to make biases visible and show how there are barriers that result in different outcomes and opportunities for certain groups in society. In line with an activist perspective, data journalism can be a way to give voice to the voiceless. There are many examples of data journalism that exposes structural inequalities, corruption and power imbalances that would otherwise remain invisible. Often those imbalances are related to gender and intersectional aspects in society. For example, the Panama Papers exposed the offshore finance industry and showed how some of the world's most prominent figures were involved in it and how these were mostly men. Women and minority groups are disproportionally affected by the excesses of global capitalism and the concentration of wealth in the hands of a small, privileged elite.

Data journalism that takes into account these sensitivities can function as a tool for empowerment, challenging persistent imbalances and hacking gender gaps. This, however, will not be the case if the same biases are reproduced as in traditional journalism. A feminist approach is necessary to expose intersectional layers of meaning in data journalism projects and to prevent that biases inherent to databases are replicated in news stories. This awareness can already be encouraged at the level of journalism education. More and more journalism schools have started to offer training in data and computational journalism. Inclusivity and diversity in data journalism should be part of the curricula.

Iteration

Innovation is frequently described as a sequential and linear process from one moment to another. Hackers question this unidirectional view and see the construction of innovative knowledge rather as the result of continuous improvement and iteration. This is connected to the belief that knowledge and systems are never complete and always open for change. Much of this applies to the struggle for gender equality as well.

Although the growing number of women both in newsrooms and journalism education has led to optimistic views on the future of gender in journalism, it would be wrong to conclude that gender equality has been accomplished and that there is no need for further efforts for achieving equal rights in journalism. Gender developments have proven to be slow, and with a high risk of backsliding. Survey research in different countries indicates that the increase in the share of women in journalism has reached a plateau (Weaver, Beam, Brownlee, Voakes, & Wilhoit, 2007; Weaver & Wilnat, 2012; Weaver & Wu, 1998). There are gendered employment patterns that seem to be immune to change (Franks, 2013), while traditional gender barriers such as the work-family conflict and the glass ceiling stubbornly persist.

Feminist history shows that rights are never entirely attained but always have to be defended. Moving forward means being attentive to forms of backlash and mechanisms that are preventing change. My research offers insight into how new inequalities emerging in online spaces of journalism are actually an iteration of disparities already present in the offline world. Just like in offline areas, women expressing their opinions online are silenced by misogynist comments, verbal and physical threats, and sexual abuse; topics related to gender issues and feminism appear to be an especially attractive red rag for trolls, cyberstalkers and online harassers. Online misogyny intersects with racism, homophobia and ageism, which makes stories about sexual violence and forms of discrimination vulnerable to counterattacks. This is very damaging to the progress that has been made toward equality because it pushes women and minority journalists out of the profession, prevents innovative and critical ideas from being shared and restricts the empowering potential of digital spaces.

Newsrooms have to move from being passive bystanders to active allies regarding these new threats and address them through specific policies to ensure the physical and mental safety of journalists. Journalists need to be protected and supported in making complaints against online harassment. This has to go hand-in-hand with an overall vision that gender equality has to be part of the core code of the news industry. In order to combat sexism in the media industry, it is not sufficient to single out the symptoms, but it is necessary to tackle the structures surrounding gender inequality. Only then will it be possible to go from punishment to prevention and from window dressing to long-term cultural changes toward gender-equal work environments.

References

Acker, J. (1990). Hierarchies, jobs, bodies: A theory of gendered organizations. *Gender & Society*, *4*(2), 139–158.

Acker, J. (1992). Gendering organizational theory. In A. Mills & P. Tancred (Eds.), *Gendering organizational analysis* (pp. 248–260). Thousand Oaks, CA: Sage.

Aldridge, M. (2001). The paradigm contingent career? Women in regional newspaper journalism. *Sociological Research Online*, *6*(3). Retrieved from www.socresonline.org.uk/6/3/aldridge.

Brooke, S. J. (2018). *Breaking gender code: Hackathons, gender, and the social dynamics of competitive creation.* Retrieved from http://hackathonworkshop-2018.com/

Byerly, C. M. (2011). *The global report on the status of women in news media.* Washington, DC: International Women's Media Foundation.

Byerly, C. M., & Ross, K. (2006). *Women & media: A critical introduction.* Malden, MA: Blackwell Publishing.

Criado-Perez, C. (2019). *Invisible women: Data bias in a world designed for men.* New York, NY: Abrams Press.

EIGE. (2013). *Review of the implementation of the Beijing platform for action in the EU member states: Women and the media – Advancing gender equality in decision-making in media organisations.* Luxembourg: Publications Office of the European Union.

Franks, S. (2013). *Women and journalism.* London, UK and New York, NY: I.B. Tauris & Co.

GMMP. (2015). *Who makes the news? Global Media Monitoring Project.* London, UK: World Association for Christian Communication.

Himanen, P. (2001). *The hacker ethic and the spirit of the information age.* London, UK: Vintage.

International Center for Journalists. (2017). *The state of technology in global newsrooms.* Retrieved from www.icfj.org/sites/default/files/2018-04/ICFJTech-SurveyFINAL.pdf

Löfgren-Nilsson, M. (2010). 'Thinkings' and 'doings' of gender: Gendering processes in Swedish television news production. *Journalism Practice*, *4*(1), 1–16.

Peters, C., & Broersma, M. J. (2013). *Rethinking journalism: Trust and participation in a transformed news landscape*. New York, NY: Routledge.

Shaw, S. (2014). The internet is full of jerks, because the world is full of jerks: What feminist theory teaches us about the internet. *Communication and Critical/Cultural Studies*, *11*(3), 273–277.

SSL Nagbot. (2016). Feminist hacking/making: Exploring new gender horizons of possibility. *Journal of Peer Production*, *8*. Retrieved from http://peerproduction.net/issues/issue-8-feminism-and-unhacking-2/

Storm, H., Posetti, J., Ziomecka, Z., Barnathan, J., Kapur, R., Kopel, O., Omar, Y., Narisetti, R., Santos, M., & Carvalho, C. (2018, June). *How to end misogyny in the news industry: An open letter to the international journalism community*. Retrieved from https://www.icfj.org/news/how-end-misogyny-news-industry-open-letter-international-journalism-community

Usher, N. (2016). *Interactive journalism: Hackers, data, and code*. Urbana, IL: University of Illinois Press.

Weaver, D. H., Beam, R. A., Brownlee, B. J., Voakes, P. S., & Wilhoit, C. G. (2007). *The American journalist in the 21st century: U.S. news people at the dawn of a new millennium*. Mahwah, NJ: Erlbaum Associated.

Weaver, D. H., & Wilnat, L. (2012). *The global journalist in the 21st century*. New York, NY: Routledge.

Weaver, D. H., & Wu, W. (1998). *The global journalist: News people around the world*. Cresskill, NJ: Hampton Press.

Index